REVISE AQA GCSE (9–1)
History
BRITAIN: HEALTH AND THE PEOPLE, c1000 to the present day

REVISION
GUIDE AND WORKBOOK

Series Consultant: Harry Smith

Author: Julia Robertson

Also available to support your revision:

Revise GCSE Study Skills Guide   9781447967071

The **Revise GCSE Study Skills Guide** is full of tried-and-trusted hints and tips for how to learn more effectively. It gives you techniques to help you achieve your best – throughout your GCSE studies and beyond!

REVISE GCSE
Study Skills
GUIDE

Revise GCSE Revision Planner   9781447967828

The **Revise GCSE Revision Planner** helps you to plan and organise your time, step-by-step, throughout your GCSE revision. Use this book and wall chart to mastermind your revision.

REVISE GCSE
REVISION PLANNER

For the full range of Pearson revision titles across KS2, KS3, GCSE, Functional Skills, AS/A Level and BTEC visit: www.pearsonschools.co.uk/revise

Contents

SUBJECT CONTENT

c1000–present
1   Health and the people

Medicine stands still

Medieval medicine
2   Approaches to disease
3   The medieval doctor

Medical progress
4   Medieval hospitals
5   Religion and medieval medicine
6   Surgery in medieval times

Public health in the Middle Ages
7   Towns and monasteries
8   The Black Death

The beginnings of change

The Renaissance
9   Vesalius, Paré and Harvey

Dealing with disease
10   Traditional and new methods of treatment
11   The Great Plague
12   Growth of hospitals

Prevention of disease
13   Inoculation and vaccination

A revolution in medicine

Germ theory
14   Pasteur
15   Koch and microbe hunting
16   Germ theory and vaccination
17   Ehrlich and magic bullets
18   Germ theory and everyday medicine

Revolution in surgery
19   Anaesthetics
20   Antiseptics and aseptic surgery

Improvements in public health
21   Industrial Britain
22   Public health reformers
23   Government involvement

Modern medicine

Modern treatment of disease
24   Developments in drugs
25   New diseases and treatments

Impact of war and technology
26   Developments in surgery

Modern public health
27   Liberal social reforms
28   Impact of war
29   The Welfare State and the NHS
30   Healthcare in the 21st century

SKILLS
31   Exam overview
32   Source skills 1
33   Source skills 2
34   Source A
35   Question 1: evaluating usefulness
36   Question 2: explaining significance
37   Question 3: making comparisons
38   Question 4: making a judgement 1
39   Question 4: making a judgement 2

PRACTICE
40   Practice questions

ANSWERS
50   Answers

....

A small bit of small print

AQA publishes Sample Assessment Material and the Specification on its website. This is the official content and this book should be used in conjunction with it. The questions in *Now try this* have been written to help you practise every topic in the book. Remember: the real exam questions may not look like this.

Health and the people

For your AQA GCSE History Paper 2 thematic study, you need to know about a time period. For this thematic study, Health and the people, the time period is just over a thousand years. There was a lot of change over this time so this timeline will help you place it all. You will also need to know a little bit about the time before the year 1000, which is why this timeline starts earlier.

Timeline

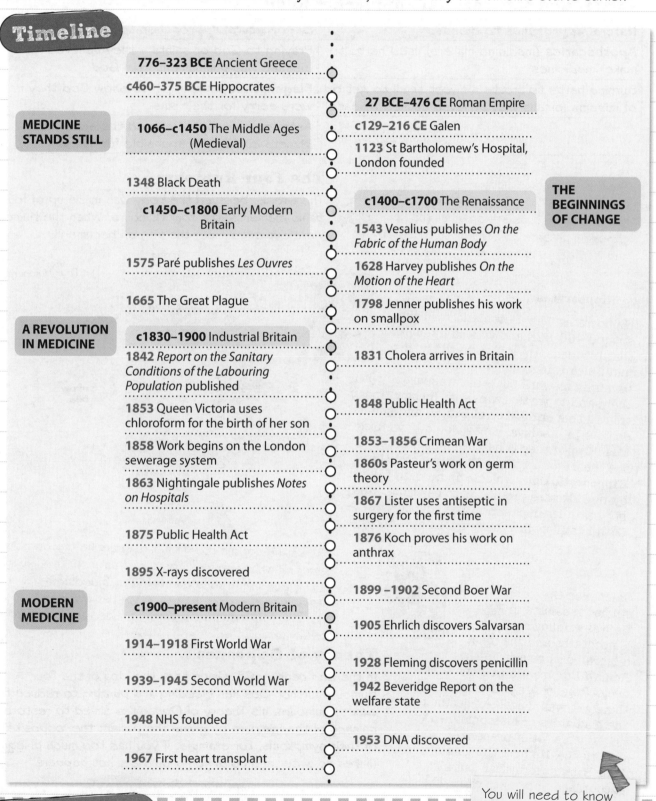

MEDICINE STANDS STILL

776–323 BCE Ancient Greece

c460–375 BCE Hippocrates

1066–c1450 The Middle Ages (Medieval)

1348 Black Death

c1450–c1800 Early Modern Britain

1575 Paré publishes *Les Ouvres*

1665 The Great Plague

A REVOLUTION IN MEDICINE

c1830–1900 Industrial Britain

1842 *Report on the Sanitary Conditions of the Labouring Population* published

1853 Queen Victoria uses chloroform for the birth of her son

1858 Work begins on the London sewerage system

1863 Nightingale publishes *Notes on Hospitals*

1875 Public Health Act

1895 X-rays discovered

MODERN MEDICINE

c1900–present Modern Britain

1914–1918 First World War

1939–1945 Second World War

1948 NHS founded

1967 First heart transplant

27 BCE–476 CE Roman Empire

c129–216 CE Galen

1123 St Bartholomew's Hospital, London founded

c1400–c1700 The Renaissance

1543 Vesalius publishes *On the Fabric of the Human Body*

1628 Harvey publishes *On the Motion of the Heart*

1798 Jenner publishes his work on smallpox

1831 Cholera arrives in Britain

1848 Public Health Act

1853–1856 Crimean War

1860s Pasteur's work on germ theory

1867 Lister uses antiseptic in surgery for the first time

1876 Koch proves his work on anthrax

1899–1902 Second Boer War

1905 Ehrlich discovers Salvarsan

1928 Fleming discovers penicillin

1942 Beveridge Report on the welfare state

1953 DNA discovered

THE BEGINNINGS OF CHANGE

You will need to know these significant dates.

Now try this

Look, cover, check. Once you have read this timeline, cover it up and see how much of it you can reproduce.

Approaches to disease

Methods of treatment and diagnosis of disease were not very reliable in Medieval Britain. Most explanations and treatments were based on supernatural approaches, although some came from ideas from the Ancient world, particularly the work of Hippocrates and Galen.

Natural and supernatural approaches to disease

Natural approaches to disease	Supernatural approaches to disease
Apothecaries (medicine-makers) used herbs to make 'medicines'	Praying to God or saints – they believed disease was punishment from God
Burning herbs to create a sweet smell to get rid of **miasma** (smells they believed caused disease)	**Flagellation** (whipping) – to show God they were sorry for their sins
For more on miasma, turn to page 21.	Astrology – people believed the stars and planets could be responsible for illness

The idea had some merit as it was rational – based on evidence from observing patients rather than on superstition – but the remedies prescribed were often unhelpful, and it hindered development in medicine.

Hippocrates

Hippocrates was a Greek doctor born around 460 BCE and was so influential that his ideas are still used today. His main idea was to observe patients carefully to work out what was wrong with them and to write down what he saw. Today we call this **clinical observation** and some doctors in medieval times would have used this. Hippocrates is best remembered for the theory of the **Four Humours** and the **Hippocratic Oath** which was an oath taken by new doctors promising to be ethical and not harm their patients. The Hippocratic Oath is still sworn today by all new doctors.

Galen

Galen was Greek but studied medicine in Egypt. He was a follower of Hippocrates and the most celebrated physician in the Roman Empire. He was the first doctor to encourage dissection even though it was illegal. As doctor to the gladiators of his hometown, he gained a lot of practical experience. He took the idea of the Four Humours further, but also encouraged doctors to check their patient's pulse for signs of what might be wrong. He wrote many books, which were edited by Islamic scholars in the medieval period.

Turn to page 5 for more on medieval Islamic medicine.

The Four Humours

The Greeks believed the body was made up of four basic elements, the Four Humours. When the Humours were out of balance, the person became ill.

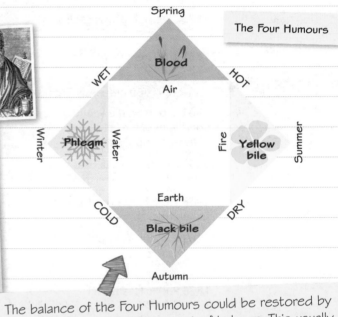

The Four Humours

Spring · WET · Blood · Air · HOT · Winter · Phlegm · Water · Fire · Yellow bile · Summer · COLD · Earth · Black bile · DRY · Autumn

The balance of the Four Humours could be restored by reducing whichever one was out of balance. This usually meant **purging** (making them sick) or **bleeding** a patient using leeches or cutting to reduce the amount of blood in their body. This idea continued until the 19th century.

Theory of Opposites

In the 2nd century CE, Galen took the idea of the Four Humours further. Besides bleeding and purging to reduce the excess humours, his Theory of Opposites aimed to restore the balance of the humours by giving the patient the 'opposite' of their symptoms. For example, if you had too much phlegm (linked to water and cold) you should eat hot peppers.

Now try this

State **one** natural and **one** supernatural approach to disease in Medieval Britain.

The medieval doctor

Medieval doctors continued to use the medical ideas of Hippocrates and Galen. There was also some progress during the medieval period, such as the establishment of new universities of physicians.

Hippocrates and Galen

- Most medieval doctors would have accepted Hippocrates' **Theory of the Four Humours** and Galen's **Theory of Opposites** without question.
- Unfortunately these weren't always useful and patients got worse.
- Most doctors still believed in supernatural causes for disease.

To revise Hippocrates and Galen, turn to page 2.

Methods of treatment

Some medieval doctors would carry a toolkit for treating people, including:

- ☑ the **vademecum** (go-with-me) diagnosis book
- ☑ **leeches** for balancing the humour of blood
- ☑ **posies** and other highly smelling objects to ward off miasma (the smells they believed caused disease)
- ☑ **herbs** for mixing natural remedies
- ☑ a **zodiac chart** to predict illnesses and suggest cures.

Training

New universities of physicians were set up in places like Bologna and Padua. At Padua students had to visit sick people as part of their training. At these schools doctors debated the best treatments for diseases and even began to watch people dissect bodies to better understand how they worked. The medieval period also saw some licensing for doctors returning from the new medical schools. New books were being produced for them to read by scholars such as **Rhazes**.

Turn to page 5 for more on Rhazes.

Training is a good example of the small seeds of change in this period.

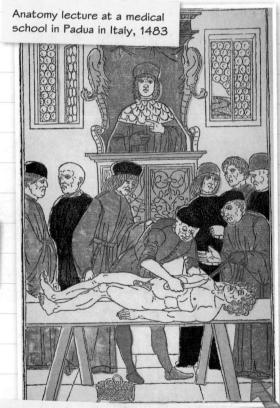

Anatomy lecture at a medical school in Padua in Italy, 1483

Observation

Medieval approaches weren't completely unscientific. Some doctors followed Hippocrates' methods and observed their patients in an effort to understand what was wrong with them. Doctors might try to work out what was wrong by taking their patient's pulse or tasting their urine. Battlefield surgeons like **Arderne** were starting to take a more scientific approach.

Turn to page 6 for more about the battlefield and barber surgeons.

Notice that in the image the professor stays in his chair and the students aren't taking part in the dissection. Dissection would have been done by a low-paid employee. Doctors were encouraged to learn by reading the books of Hippocrates and Galen, not by hands-on activities like dissecting and experimenting.

Now try this

List **three** examples of signs of progress in the work of medieval doctors.

Medieval hospitals

Most sick people were cared for at home by their female relatives but, for the first time since the Roman era, hospitals were now being built and used. These hospitals were very different to those of today: often they didn't treat the sick but just offered **hospitality** to travellers and pilgrims (which is how they got their name).

Funding mainly came from rich donors' **endowments**.

An **endowment** is a large amount of money given to pay for setting up and continuing support.

The Church wanted to show people that charity could help cure disease and earn you a place in heaven.

The emphasis in hospitals was on **care rather than cure**.

Hospitals and patients were kept very clean.

Most patients had to share a bed unless they were very close to death.

Hospitals in Medieval Britain

The number of hospitals increased during the medieval period for the first time since the Roman Empire.

Pregnant women and people with infectious diseases weren't usually admitted.

Some specialist hospitals were built for patients with infectious diseases or mental health problems.

About a third of hospitals were set up by the **Church** and run by monks and nuns.

The Hotel Dieu, Paris

Examples of medieval hospitals

✓ **Bedlam**, London, is one of the oldest mental hospitals in the world. It was founded by the Christian Church in 1247 to look after homeless people but before long began to focus on people who were considered 'mad'.

✓ The **Hotel Dieu** in Paris is one of Europe's oldest hospitals. It was founded in 651 by Saint Landry. It offered medical care as well as food and shelter for the sick and poor. At its busiest patients would be six to a bed.

Now try this

Look at the image on the right. What does it tell you about who set up medieval hospitals and why? Identify **two** points and use the information on this page to find reasons.

Think about the religious beliefs of the time.

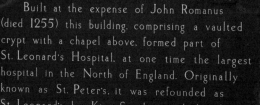

ST. LEONARD'S HOSPITAL

Built at the expense of John Romanus (died 1255) this building, comprising a vaulted crypt with a chapel above, formed part of St. Leonard's Hospital, at one time the largest hospital in the North of England. Originally known as St. Peter's, it was refounded as St. Leonard's by King Stephen and dissolved in 1540.

Plaque at the medieval St Leonard's Hospital, York

Religion and medieval medicine

Medieval medicine in Britain and the **Christian Church** were very closely linked. The effect was mainly negative but there were some positives. Medicine in the medieval **Muslim** world was very different and made bigger leaps forward.

Christianity and medicine: negatives

- The most negative impact that the Christian Church had on medicine was the belief in supernatural causes of illness.

- The Church taught that disease was a **punishment** from God for sin.

- People were encouraged to rely on **prayers** to cure them.

- This meant that doctors didn't make the effort to investigate new ideas about the causes of disease or new treatments.

- Dissection of human corpses was forbidden, so many wrong ideas about **anatomy** continued.

- The Church insisted that people believe in the work of Galen without question.

- The emphasis was on **care**, not **cure**.

- Religious wars like the **Crusades** cost a lot of money, which might otherwise have been spent on public health.

The contribution of Christianity to medical progress

The Christian Church's role in medicine wasn't all negative:

- The Church set up and ran most of the new hospitals, like the Hotel Dieu in Paris.

To see more about hospitals, turn to page 4.

- Encouraging people to go on wars like the **Crusades** to the Middle East put them in touch with Muslim doctors who were much more skilled and knowledgeable.

Islamic medicine

During the reign of **Harun al-Rashid** (786–809) Islamic medicine and surgery really moved forward. The books of **Hippocrates** and **Galen** were translated into Arabic by doctors like Al-Razi (also known as **Rhazes**), who preserved their ideas. Later, Islamic doctors such as **Ibn al-Nafis** started to challenge the ideas of the Ancients. Knowledge was slow to get to Britain but one book, the *Canon of Medicine* by Ibn Sina (also known as **Avicenna**), spread quickly. Islamic medicine was the first to have pharmacies and a system of weighing and measuring ingredients in medicines was invented.

The medieval period was the first time that **pharmacy** (the science of preparing and giving out medicines) was seen as separate to medicine.

Developments in medieval Muslim medicine reached Britain via European doctors coming home from the **Crusades**.

The Crusades put many European doctors in touch with the ideas and practices of Muslim doctors like Avicenna.

You can use this topic to talk about the roles **superstition**, **religion** and **war** played in moving medicine back and moving it forward.

Now try this

Make a list of **two** ways the Christian Church in the medieval period held medicine back, and **two** ways in which it moved things forward.

Surgery in medieval times

Surgery made some great progress in medieval times. In Europe, this was thanks to **barber surgeons** treating battlefield injuries. Islamic surgery made great leaps forward and recorded knowledge was shared. Useful discoveries in **antiseptics** and pain control were made during this time.

Bleeding – patients would often bleed to death.

Infection – doctors had no idea that dirt carried disease.

Problems in medieval surgery

Pain control – new methods were often so strong they would kill the patient.

Shock – patients' bodies would go into shock because of pain or blood loss.

Medieval surgeons

- Medieval surgeons weren't surgeons as we would think of them today. Most were 'barber surgeons' who travelled the country treating soldiers who had been wounded in battle. They also did simple procedures such as tooth extractions and bloodletting.

- Surgeons didn't have any formal training and mainly learned on the job, apprenticed to other surgeons. At this time, women couldn't become doctors but could become surgeons, as it was considered to be a lower profession.

Al-Zahrawi's work helped move surgery in Britain forward when doctors returning from the Crusades brought back his ideas and books.

Arderne wrote books (such as *The Practice of Surgery*, 1370) about his work which were widely read by surgeons at the time. It also advised doctors on how to behave.

Hugh and Theodoric wrote many books on surgery, challenging other surgeons' traditional methods.

Early successes in surgery

Al-Zahrawi (Albucasis) was a famous Islamic surgeon and doctor born around 936 CE. He had a lot of experience treating war casualties and wrote many important books on surgery, including how to treat battlefield injuries. He even invented new surgical instruments. His books and ideas were used for many centuries by both Islamic and Western doctors and surgeons.

John Arderne, said to be the first English surgeon, worked as a surgeon on the battlefields where he developed his own pain-killing ointment made from hemlock and opium.

Hugh of Lucca was a famous surgeon who served in the army during the Crusades and noticed that wine was very good for cleaning wounds. Other surgeons used **cauterisation** (burning the wound), which was ineffective against infection. Hugh and his son Theodoric observed patients and saw that pus in wounds was harmful, whereas other surgeons thought it was good for cleaning the blood. We know now that pus is a sign of infection.

Medieval surgeons worked out how to use alcohol as an **antiseptic** (to clean away germs).

Alcohol and herbs such as hemlock or opium were used as simple **pain control**.

You need to know how key factors **combine** to change things. This topic combines war and the role of the individual.

Progress in medieval surgery

New instruments and techniques were developed as a result of treating soldiers' battle wounds from the many wars at the time.

Some complicated surgery became possible, including mending a broken skull.

Now try this

Write a short paragraph explaining how war helped Al-Zahrawi move surgery forward.

Towns and monasteries

Medieval towns weren't always very clean but they took some measures to improve **public health**. Religious houses were cleaner. People knew there was a connection between being clean and having good health, even if they did not know the scientific reasons behind it.

Lifestyle in a medieval town

Medieval towns were very unhealthy places to live.

- A lot of people lived so close together that diseases spread very quickly.
- There were no sewers and no rules for getting rid of waste.
- Most people got their water from streams and rivers, which were often **contaminated** with human waste that was just thrown into the streets.
- Where there were water wells, **cesspits** (pits for the disposal of sewage) were often built close by, so this water was contaminated too.
- Butchers slaughtered their animals in the streets and left the waste.
- Towns were usually so dirty that they smelled very bad. This is why **miasma** (bad smell) was believed to be the cause of disease.
- Some **councils** did try to clean up towns, although they weren't clear about the effects this could have on public health.

Some towns were better than others at trying to make public health better. **Leadership**, **money** and **initiative** were the biggest factors in whether a town was successful.

Lifestyle in a medieval monastery

Most medieval monasteries were much cleaner than towns.

- Usually, monks and nuns knew it was best to take water from upstream for drinking, brewing and washing, rather than from downstream where it would be **contaminated** by water from the toilets.
- Monasteries often had running water systems and **sewers**.
- Monks and nuns were usually the only medical practitioners in the area and would have to keep their cupboards well stocked with herbs and wine for treating the sick.
- Most hospitals were attached to religious houses at this time and monks and nuns would work in both the monastery and the hospital as part of their Christian duty.
- Monasteries were often kept very clean. The monks and nuns understood the importance of cleanliness for health even if they did not know the science behind it.
- As most hospitals were attached to and run by religious houses, monasteries would grow herbs in their **physic garden** and a **herbalist** or **apothecary** would offer the herbs to patients for treatment.

For more on medieval hospitals, turn to page 4.

Some medieval towns like Coventry, shown in this picture, did make efforts to clean up. The town council banned dumping rubbish in the streets and river, and in 1421 ordered that all toilets built over a local stream had to be demolished.

This is a good piece of information for talking about the **role of government** in public health, as it shows that local government was trying to change things even in Medieval times.

Now try this

Write **two** sentences to describe the role of government in public health in the Middle Ages.

The Black Death

The Black Death was an **epidemic** (outbreak of disease that becomes widespread) that first came to Britain in 1348 and killed thousands of people. Most people believed it was caused by supernatural factors and treatment and prevention were mainly based on these ideas.

What was it?

The **Black Death** was actually an outbreak of the **bubonic plague**. It is called this because the main symptom is **buboes** (swellings) in the groin and armpit. Other symptoms are fever and coughing up blood. There was no cure and most of those who caught the disease died within days. The bacteria that caused it were actually carried by infected fleas that came into the country on rats on ships. Dirty conditions in towns meant that it spread quickly and easily.

What did people think caused it?

- **Supernatural** explanations: punishment from God for sin; misalignment of the planets.
- **Natural** explanations: miasma; imbalance of the Humours.

Medical knowledge about the causes of disease hadn't advanced beyond these widely believed explanations.

Social and economic impact

☑ **Rich and poor** – being rich was no guarantee of protection and the disease killed **30–45 per cent** of the population. In some villages it killed 100 per cent.

☑ **Panic** – in some places the Black Death caused panic and **rioting**. In Durham in 1349 the epidemic combined with the threat of invasion by the Scots led to a mass riot in the town.

☑ **Society the wrong way up** – within a year government passed **the Statute of Labourers** to try to stop the peasants who were left from demanding higher wages. A few years later they tried to pass a law telling people what they could wear and eat, with the aim of keeping the peasants 'in their place'.

☑ **Religion** – the Black Death had killed lots of religious clergy too: replacements were hard to find and many churches were left empty. Where new clergy were found, they often demanded much higher wages.

For more about the reasons why people believed these explanations, and the Four Humours, turn to page 2.

Treatment and prevention

Supernatural	Natural
Pray for forgiveness of sins	Correct the imbalance of the Humours through bleeding and purging (this actually made things worse)
Accept God's will	Smelling or setting fire to strong smelling herbs and boiling vinegar to avoid the miasma
Self-flagellation (whipping yourself to show God how sorry you are for your sins)	Escape!

Now try this

Explain how this image helps understanding of the part religion and superstition played in the Black Death.

Think about what people thought caused the Black Death.

Flagellants whipping themselves to try to avoid getting the Black Death

Vesalius, Paré and Harvey

During the Renaissance there were some important individuals who really challenged authority in **anatomy** (study of the make-up of the human body), **physiology** (study of the workings of the human body) and surgery. **Vesalius, Paré** and **Harvey** made new discoveries with a big impact but not everybody welcomed their ideas and there was a lot of opposition to change.

The Renaissance (c1400–c1700)

- The Renaissance was a time of new ideas and interest. New scientific ideas started to have an impact on medicine and public health.

- In 1440 the **printing press** was invented, meaning that new ideas could spread much more rapidly, especially with new universities being set up all around Europe.

- New thinkers, led by **Paracelsus** (1493–1541), began to challenge the work of Hippocrates and Galen.

- In the 1600s people started doing experiments to prove that the old ideas were wrong.

Andreas Vesalius

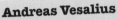

Vesalius studied medicine in Padua where he later became Professor of Anatomy and Surgery. He was convinced that anatomy was the best way to understand the human body and unlike people before him he did his own **dissections**. In his book *On the Fabric of the Human Body*, 1543, he corrected over 300 of Galen's mistakes and argued the importance of doctors learning from dissections rather than books.

Opposition to change

Some people embraced more scientific methods but others were not convinced. Many people did not agree with experimenting to prove theories and there were still many people who believed in Galen's work and were reluctant to accept that he might have been wrong. English textbooks for doctors continued to publish the ideas of Galen until the 1650s and people like Harvey were ridiculed for their ideas at the time. In everyday medicine very little changed.

Ambroise Paré

Ambroise Paré was a barber surgeon who learned much of what he knew from being an army surgeon. He invented a new way of sealing wounds on the battlefield and used **ligatures** to tie blood vessels for the first time.

William Harvey

Harvey studied medicine in Padua and came back to England in 1602 as a physician. He was interested in **physiology**, particularly blood, and using experiments and dissection he proved that blood circulates around the body using **arteries** and **veins** with valves. He also showed that the heart acted as a pump for the system. His understanding of the **circulatory system** is the basis of what we know today but it took many years for his ideas to be accepted.

Despite so many new ideas coming forward between c1500 and c1700 it would be a long time before they made a difference to day-to-day medicine and public health.

Remember, the role of individuals is one of the key factors you need to be able to talk about in the exam.

Microscopes began to be developed during the Renaissance. In 1665 the book *Micrographia* by **Robert Hooke** showed detailed images from magnified images for the first time and by 1683 microscopes were made more powerful by **Antonie van Leeuwenhoek**.

The impact of their discoveries was felt in Britain, for example, through people like Thomas Geminus and William Clowes.

Now try this

Name **two** things that Vesalius, Paré and Harvey all had in common.

Traditional and new methods of treatment

The Renaissance had brought some new treatments but most people still had to rely on doctors who had little or no training such as **quacks** (dishonest medical practitioners) and barber surgeons.

Turn to page 6 for more on barber surgeons.

Methods of treatment

Traditional approaches	New approaches
Religious, such as praying for forgiveness, pilgrimage and giving money to the Church	Growing number of hospitals, which started to treat the sick rather than just providing hospitality
Wise women, who used herbs and charms	Many towns had a pharmacy
Herbal remedies	New herbs and ingredients from around the world
Astrology	Books on medicine for treating the family at home
Quackery	Scientific approaches

King's Evil and the Royal Touch: It was believed that the touch of a royal (particularly the king) could cure the skin disease scrofula which was known as 'King's Evil'.

Quackery

- **Quackery** (dishonest medical practice) had always happened but in the 17th and 18th centuries there was a huge increase. During the Great Plague of 1665 quack doctors were widespread.

For more on the Great Plague, turn to page 11.

- Quacks sold their own medicines, which they said would prevent or cure disease, knowing they would have no effect. Most were travelling salesmen who moved on before people realised this.

'Operation for Stones in the Head'. A quack doctor pretends to cure a woman of insanity by making a cut in her head and pretending to take out stones which are actually passed to him by his helper standing behind her.

- Quack medicines were often a combination of alcohol and opium, which sometimes gave patients the impression that they were getting better, but made no difference at all.

The new scientific approach

- A new emphasis on a scientific approach to medicine led to some new medical ideas.
- In 1753, **James Lind** carried out the first ever **clinical trials** (research studies with a group of human participants).

James Lind found that the disease **scurvy** could be cured by eating fresh fruit and vegetables, in particular citrus fruits.

Now try this

Cover up the table above and then list **three traditional** and **three new** approaches to treatment during the Renaissance.

The Great Plague

The Great Plague of 1665 was the worst outbreak of the plague in Britain since the Black Death in 1348. There were some differences in how people tried to prevent and treat it, but things hadn't changed much.

What was it?

In **1665** the **bubonic plague** returned to Britain. As with the Black Death of 1348, it was caused by the *Yersinia pestis* germ, which lived in the digestive system of fleas. The fleas were carried by rats, which were attracted to the cramped and dirty conditions in towns, meaning that the germs spread very quickly. At its worst point in September 1665 over 7000 people died in one week in London.

Turn to page 8 for more on the bubonic plague (Black Death).

A woodcut from 1665 showing the Great Plague with the title 'Lord Have Mercy on London'. It shows that most people still believed that the disease was a punishment from God. London lost around 15 per cent of its population, with 68 596 recorded deaths (the actual total was probably nearer 100 000).

Beliefs about causes

- People still didn't really understand what was causing the plague.
- They still believed it was a punishment from God.
- They believed that disease could be caused by miasma.
- For the first time it was noticed that people living in the poorer (and therefore dirtier) areas of the city were worst affected.

Treatments

- Balancing the **humours** by bleeding patients with leeches.
- Burning herbs to try to banish the foul air.
- Sniffing sponges soaked in vinegar.

(In reality none of these worked and bleeding actually made it worse.)

Preventative measures

- Trade with affected towns was stopped.
- Infected houses were locked up by guards.
- The border with Scotland was closed.
- The king published very strict orders about the movement of people and animals, treatment of infected houses and where people could be buried.
- Plague doctors wore special suits with sweet-smelling herbs in the nose to protect them against miasma and **amulets** (jewellery or ornaments) to ward off evil spirits.

Comparing the Great Plague to the Black Death is a good way to show continuity and change.

The Lord Mayor's Orders

The Lord Mayor's Orders were designed to stop the spread of the plague in London in 1665 and included:

- people employed to kill stray cats and dogs
- plague graves at least six feet deep and no public gatherings around them
- searchers to identify houses where people had died of the plague
- two watchmen to supervise an infected house to stop people going in or out.

Although the number of deaths continued to rise, some think that it would have been even worse without some of these measures.

Now try this

Using this page and page 8, compare the Great Plague with the Black Death by choosing **three** things they had in common.

11

Growth of hospitals

The late 18th and early 19th centuries saw big changes in hospitals, which began to change focus from care to treatment and learning. Important hospital reformers, such as **Florence Nightingale**, also made a big difference. The training and status of surgeons changed in this period too.

For more on earlier hospitals, turn to page 4.

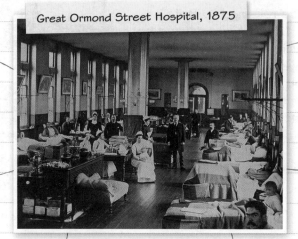

Great Ormond Street Hospital, 1875

Due to the work of reformers like Florence Nightingale, hospital cleanliness and organisation improved, and nurses were better trained. Pasteur's germ theory led to improved hygiene.

Public pressure led to infirmaries (separate from workhouses) being set up for the poorest in society.

Nurses were given a more central role caring for patients and assisting doctors. They were also trained for the first time, often alongside doctors, in hospitals.

Specialist hospitals (such as asylums for the mentally ill and fever houses for infectious diseases) developed.

Many new hospitals were built. By 1860, London alone had 36 specialist hospitals.

Hospitals now trained doctors and surgeons and often had a dispensary for preparing and giving out medicines.

Florence Nightingale

Florence Nightingale was significant in bringing about change in hospitals. After witnessing high death rates in military hospitals during the Crimean War, she challenged methods, especially at Scutari. Changes developed during her time there later saw death rates plummet from 42% to 2%. Her work was widely reported in newspapers and she published books such as *Notes on Nursing* and *Notes on Hospitals*, which discussed hospital organisation.

After her experience in military hospitals, Florence Nightingale went on to set up Britain's first nurse training school.

Wars were much bigger than they had been and weapons were more destructive so doctors needed better training and skills to cope with this.

John Hunter

Hunter was a Scottish surgeon who started off working for his brother who was a successful doctor. He was heavily interested in dissection and gifted at anatomy. In 1760 he became an army surgeon and saw many casualties in war.

Hunter set up a practice which trained many new doctors (including Edward Jenner). Hunter is known as the 'father of scientific surgery'.

Now try this

Compare medieval hospitals with hospitals in the late 18th and early 19th centuries by identifying **two** similarities.

Inoculation and vaccination

Smallpox is a **contagious** disease – a disease spread from one person to another through direct contact. It was widespread in Britain in the 18th century and spread very quickly, killing many people. Ideas about what caused disease were starting to change and people like Edward Jenner began to look for new ways of preventing disease, eventually coming up with **vaccination**.

Timeline

The smallpox vaccination

1796 Jenner tests his theory by inserting pus taken from the cowpox pustule of a milkmaid into a cut on a young boy's arm. Days later the boy is exposed to smallpox and is shown to be **immune** (resistant).

1798 Jenner finally publishes his idea.

1807 Jenner is offered more government money.

1840 Vaccination against smallpox made free to all children.

1796 Major outbreak kills around 35 000.

1797 Jenner tries to publish his findings but is told he hasn't enough evidence. He continues to experiment (including on his own baby).

1802 Jenner is awarded money from the government to research the idea further.

1837 Major outbreak kills around 42 000.

1853 Vaccination against smallpox made compulsory in England and Wales.

Vaccination originally meant giving someone a weakened dose of cowpox to protect them against smallpox. Today it means exposing the body to a weakened version of a microorganism that can cause disease, to develop immunity.

Smallpox

- Smallpox was one of the world's greatest killers and most feared diseases. There is evidence of its existence in Ancient Egypt.

- By the 17th and 18th centuries smallpox was **endemic** (regularly found) in Britain.

- The symptoms started with high fever followed by pustules on the skin.

- The disease was highly contagious and at one time around 60 per cent of people who caught it would die. Even if you survived you could be left blind and would definitely be left with terrible scars.

- Smallpox was finally **eradicated** (eliminated) in 1980 after a huge vaccination campaign all over the world.

Reasons for opposition to change

- People who charged to provide inoculations were worried they would lose income.

- People thought smallpox was a punishment from God and should just be accepted.

- Cowpox was a disease of cattle and people thought it was unnatural to put an animal disease into humans.

In 1866 the Anti-Compulsory Vaccination League was set up to protest against the idea of forced vaccination.

Years later Jenner's work was taken seriously and vaccination against smallpox was made compulsory.

Edward Jenner

Edward Jenner (1749–1823) was a country doctor who studied medicine in London. As a doctor he had **inoculated** patients against smallpox.

Working in the country, Jenner had heard that milkmaids didn't catch smallpox and set out to discover why. He discovered that they did catch **cowpox** (a much milder disease than smallpox) and reasoned that this must make them immune to smallpox. He experimented and proved this was true, calling his new idea vaccination.

Now try this

Write a paragraph including **three** reasons why people were opposed to Jenner's work.

Inoculation means deliberately infecting with a disease to avoid a more severe case of it later.

Pasteur

The 19th century saw great changes in understanding about the causes of disease. The discovery by **Pasteur** that **germs** (bacteria) caused disease changed everything. This became known as **germ theory**.

Spontaneous generation

Before Pasteur discovered that germs cause disease, doctors had realised that bacteria existed but thought that the disease caused the bacteria, not the other way round. This was called the theory of **spontaneous generation**.

Microorganisms, or **microbes**, are tiny organisms. **Germs** are an example of microorganisms.

Louis Pasteur

Pasteur was a French chemist who used experiments with beer and milk to discover small organisms that made these liquids go off, which he called germs. He invented **pasteurisation** by working out that a lot of these germs could be killed off by heating them. His work went on to be used by him and other scientists to develop vaccinations and **magic bullets**.

For more on vaccination, including Pasteur's role, turn to page 16. For more on magic bullets, turn to page 17.

Living **microorganisms** are found in the air.

Heating **microbes** can kill them.

Germ theory

Decay is caused by microbes in the air.

Remember that most people still believed that miasma, God, astrology or an imbalance of the Four Humours caused disease. Germ theory eventually changed this, but it took a long time for the idea to be accepted and even longer for it to change the way medicine was practised.

Germ theory

- Germ theory was a major breakthrough. Through a combination of **experimental science** and the **role of individuals**, the way that people thought about and treated disease was changed forever.

- Pasteur was first to uncover the link between germs and disease. He saw that microbes in the air caused disease and that if they could be identified then vaccines could be produced to target specific diseases.

- Pasteur mainly worked in food and drink, so it was the work of later doctors and surgeons which really got germ theory accepted.

For more on germ theory, turn to page 16.

The importance of Pasteur

- Pasteur's work on germ theory didn't have much impact on medicine in Britain at first, as he wasn't a doctor and his work was based on studies of beer, not disease.

- Most doctors continued to believe the theory of spontaneous generation. While Pasteur's studies laid the foundations, it was the work of people like **Koch** and **Lister** that resulted in germ theory being accepted.

You can read more about Koch on page 15 and about Lister on page 20.

The role of science and technology

☑ None of the new research would have been possible without the development of **microscopes**, which allowed scientists to see images of bacteria.

☑ Around the same time other inventions like the **stethoscope** (instrument for listening to the heart), the **thermometer** (instrument for measuring temperature) and the first **X-ray machines** made a big difference to how diseases were treated.

For more on the development of microscopes, turn to page 9. For more on X-rays, turn to page 26.

Now try this

Give **two** examples of how technology helped to make germ theory possible.

Koch and microbe hunting

Many great scientists used germ theory as a springboard for their own work. One example was Robert Koch, who proved that bacteria caused disease.

Robert Koch

- Koch was a German doctor who is considered to be the founder of modern **bacteriology**.
- Koch used experiments to prove that specific microorganisms (bacteria) were responsible for causing disease. He also developed a way of staining bacteria so that they could be seen under a microscope.
- He was awarded a Nobel Prize in 1905.

Public health

☑ Germ theory became very important in the debate on public health in towns and cities in 19th century Britain.

☑ Not everyone was convinced by germ theory and the work of Pasteur, or even Koch, to begin with.

☑ This played a big role in 19th century medical debate. The **contagionists** argued that disease could be spread through germs while the **anti-contagionists** held on to the theory that disease was spread by miasma.

☑ This had a big impact on the time it took for germ theory to be accepted and public health policy to improve.

For more about Ehrlich, turn to page 17.
For more about Pasteur, turn to page 14. ⟹

Koch and anthrax

- Koch used scientific experiments to prove that the germ or bacteria *Bacillus anthracis* caused anthrax.
- He took the **bacillus** from a sheep which had died of the disease and injected it into a mouse, which also caught the disease.
- Once Koch had done this many times he was able to convince people that bacteria caused disease.
- Following this discovery he was able to go on to identify the bacillus that caused **tuberculosis**. Also known as TB, tuberculosis was a highly infectious disease affecting the lungs, one of the biggest killer diseases in Britain at the time.

Pasteur   Koch   Ehrlich

The lead scientists in germ theory

Staining bacteria so it could be viewed under a microscope.

Koch himself identified the bacteria causing: anthrax (1876), septicaemia (1878), tuberculosis (TB) (1882) and cholera (1883).

Others developed **magic bullets** (chemicals that attach to germs and kill them).

For more on magic bullets, see page 17.

Discoveries made possible by Koch's work

Koch's identification of different bacteria led others to identify: typhus (1880), pneumonia (1880), tetanus (1884), diphtheria (1884) and the plague (1890).

Koch's assistant invented the Petri dish (so bacteria could be observed more easily).

Now try this

Why was Koch's work so important? Give **three** reasons.

Germ theory and vaccination

Germ theory had a huge impact on the development of vaccinations. A century after Jenner's discovery about smallpox, Pasteur found a way of creating vaccines in his lab. This would change the fight against disease forever.

You can read more about Jenner on page 13.

Timeline

The development of vaccinations

1700s Variolation (an ancient form of vaccination which originated in China) spreads to Britain.

1840 Vaccination against smallpox made free to all children.

1880 While working with Pasteur, Charles Chamberland discovers that injecting chickens with a weak form of chicken cholera gives them immunity.

1885 Pasteur discovers effective vaccine against rabies.

1913 Emil von Behring discovers anti-toxins against diphtheria and tetanus.

1955 Polio vaccination begins in the UK.

2008 NHS introduces vaccination against cervical cancer for school-age girls.

429 BCE Thucydides observes that people surviving the smallpox plague in Athens didn't get infected again.

1798 Jenner publishes his findings about smallpox vaccination.

1853 Vaccination against smallpox made compulsory in England and Wales.

1881 Pasteur discovers effective vaccine against anthrax.

1906 Albert Calmette and Camille Guérin develop the BCG injection to protect against tuberculosis.

1920s Vaccines become widely available.

1980 Smallpox eradicated through **WHO** vaccination programme.

2015 NHS vaccinates babies against meningitis B.

Pasteur and vaccination

- Pasteur had always said that germ theory would lead to a way of vaccinating against diseases.

- He started to study chicken cholera in 1879. Pasteur and Chamberland experimented by injecting chickens with an old culture of bacteria in the lab. The chickens were ill but didn't die and became immune to the disease. They had discovered that weak forms of a disease could help people develop immunity to that disease. In 1881 Pasteur began experimenting with a vaccine for **anthrax** and in 1885 with a vaccine for **rabies**.

- Pasteur took a risk and injected the vaccine he had created in the lab into a young boy bitten by an animal infected with rabies: the boy survived. The first trial of a man-made vaccine had been a success.

Germ theory paved the way for vaccines made in the lab which have gone on to **eradicate** some of the biggest killer diseases in the world.

For more on Pasteur, turn to page 14.

You don't need to know all of the dates on this timeline, but you do need to know that vaccination as we know it today took a long time to evolve.

Cartoon from 1898 commenting on a Bill of Parliament which allowed parents unsure about vaccination to opt out without penalty.

Remember not everyone was convinced by vaccination. By the 1880s there was a strong **anti-vaccination league** which still exists even today.

Now try this

What does the cartoon from 1898 (above) tell you about people's reactions to vaccination? Write a paragraph, using the cartoon and your own knowledge.

Ehrlich and magic bullets

The discovery of 'magic bullets' by Paul Ehrlich is one of the most important discoveries in treating specific diseases. It was the first time a disease could actually be cured and meant that germ theory was finally making an impact on the way people treated diseases.

Paul Ehrlich

German chemist Paul Ehrlich joined Koch's research team as a young scientist. His aim was to use his expertise in chemistry to advance medicine. It was Ehrlich who came up with the term **'chemotherapy'** and discovered the process for using chemical dyes to stain and kill **specific** bacteria but not harm anything else in a patient's body. In 1908 he was awarded the Nobel Prize in Medicine.

Ehrlich is a good example of the role of the individual in encouraging change.

Discovery

- Ehrlich started out by dyeing microorganisms so he could see them better under a microscope. He had the idea that if he could attach a chemical to germs to stain them, maybe he could find chemicals that would attach to germs and kill them.

- He called these chemicals **magic bullets** after the old superstition that a bullet could be charmed to make sure it hit the right person.

- In 1909 he found **Salvarsan**, which was a cure for **syphilis** (a sexually transmitted disease which affected huge numbers of people).

Remember it was Koch who taught Ehrlich to stain microorganisms. Without this technique magic bullets might never have been found.

By **1914** Ehrlich and his team had discovered magic bullets to kill: **syphilis**, **malaria** and **sleeping sickness**.

Impressed by their work, many other doctors and scientists, such as **Emil von Behring**, thought researchers should give up developing drugs to treat the symptoms of disease and concentrate on finding drugs to kill the disease itself.

Impact of Ehrlich's work

The work formed the foundation of the modern pharmaceutical industry.

This was also the first time anyone had really done large-scale experimenting in drug research.

For more on the pharmaceutical industry, turn to page 24.

Paul Ehrlich (left) with Sahachiro Hata. In 1909 Hata joined Ehrlich's team, bringing with him new ways of working which eventually led to them finding the first magic bullet.

Now try this

Give **three** reasons why the discovery of magic bullets was so important.

Germ theory and everyday medicine

Germ theory solved the mystery of what causes disease. It took a lot of work before it was widely accepted, but eventually had a huge impact on everyday medical treatments and remedies in Britain.

Beliefs in the 19th century

At the beginning of the 19th century, beliefs about what caused disease included:

- ✓ miasma
- ✓ spontaneous generation
- ✓ imbalance of the Four Humours
- ✓ religious or supernatural reasons.

For more on spontaneous generation, turn to page 14.

Beliefs in the 20th century

At the beginning of the 20th century, beliefs about what caused disease started to include germs.

The traditional ideas still carried on for a while but gradually everyone came to accept germ theory.

Even influential figures like Florence Nightingale believed in miasma until convinced by germ theory.

During the last twenty years of the 19th century doctors were persuaded to believe in germ theory by people such as **William Roberts** and to change their practices as a result.

Surgery became safer thanks to the work of people like **Joseph Lister** and **Sir William Cheyne**.

Hospitals become cleaner and safer thanks to the work of hospital reformers.

How treatments available to ordinary people in Britain changed

Eventually in the 20th century, germ theory would lead to the development of drugs (in particular antibiotics) to treat disease that would be available to everyone.

Developments in microscopes combined to mean that diseases could be identified more easily and quickly and could be treated with more accuracy and effect.

Vaccinations for more diseases such as anthrax and tuberculosis became available and grew in popularity; many immunisations were made mandatory for soldiers during the First World War and some diseases such as diphtheria became almost non-existent.

Local doctors would visit sick people in their homes but at a cost that many people could not afford.

The acceptance of germ theory

- ✓ The work of many people played a crucial role: Pasteur, Koch, Lister, Ehrlich, Roberts and Cheyne.
- ✓ Remember it was only **after** the work of these people and others that germ theory was accepted.
- ✓ Roberts and Cheyne in particular were vital in convincing British doctors of the importance of Koch's work.
- ✓ By the 20th century, its impact on everyday medical treatments and remedies was huge.

Now try this

Give **three** ways in which germ theory changed people's experience of medical treatment.

Anaesthetics

The two main problems surgeons were still dealing with were pain and death from infection. The second half of the 19th century saw big discoveries in both of these areas. Modern anaesthetics were pioneered by James Simpson to great effect.

Timeline

An **anaesthetic** is a substance that makes people unable to feel pain.

The development of anaesthetics

1774 Joseph Priestley publishes his work on nitrous oxide (laughing gas).

1842 Crawford Long uses ether as an anaesthetic during a complicated operation but doesn't publish his experience.

1847 James Simpson first uses ether for pain relief during childbirth.

1847 Simpson first uses chloroform in an operation.

1853 John Snow uses chloroform on Queen Victoria for the birth of her eighth child.

1884 Carl Koller discovers cocaine can be used as a **local** anaesthetic – numbing a small area rather than the whole body.

1525 Paracelsus uses ether (a gas) on animals.

1799 Sir Humphry Davy experiments on himself with nitrous oxide and discovers it makes him laugh (giving it the name laughing gas). He experiments on friends too and comes to the conclusion it could be used to dull pain.

1845 Horace Wells uses laughing gas to have one of his own teeth removed.

1847 Jean Pierre Flourens discovers that chloroform has the same effect on animals as ether.

1848 A woman in Newcastle dies from overuse of chloroform – it is widely reported in the news.

1872 Pierre-Cyprien Ore gives the first **intravenous** (injected into a vein) anaesthetic. Up to this point, gases had been breathed in.

James Simpson

Simpson (1811–1870) was an **obstetrician** (specialist in childbirth) and the pioneer of using chloroform as an anaesthetic. He became physician to Queen Victoria in 1847 and was the first person to deliver a baby using anaesthetic. He was notorious for experimenting on his friends and at one party he gave everyone a decanter of chloroform to test dose rates: the guests were found unconscious on the floor the following morning. Simpson worked tirelessly to make chloroform safer and more effective and his discovery was taken up all over Europe within weeks of him proving it worked.

Acceptance and impact

Modern anaesthetics took some time to be accepted.

✓ Some people still said that pain was a punishment from God.

✓ Most people were just frightened as many of the experimental operations using anaesthetics went wrong: patients were still able to feel everything, and in some cases died.

✓ Acceptance by people like Queen Victoria in 1853 encouraged others.

Now try this

Give **two** reasons why it took time for modern anaesthetics to be accepted.

Antiseptics and aseptic surgery

Death from infection was one of the main problems for surgery going into the 19th century. In the second half of the 19th century Lister made a huge impact with antiseptics and **aseptic surgery**.

Timeline

> **Antiseptics** are substances that prevent the growth of germs, preventing infection.

Development of antiseptics and aseptic surgery

1847 Ignaz Semmelweis makes doctors on his maternity ward wash their hands in calcium chloride, reducing the number of women and babies who die.

1863 Nightingale publishes *Notes on Hospitals* in which she talks about cleanliness in hospitals.

1890 James Halstead starts to use protective clothing (gloves, masks) during surgery, beginning aseptic surgery.

1536 Ambroise Paré uses turpentine on the battlefield to clean wounds.

1854 Florence Nightingale begins to influence standards of cleaning in hospitals.

1865 Joseph Lister begins using **carbolic acid** on surgical instruments and to cover wounds, drastically reducing deaths among his patients.

> In **aseptic surgery**, germs are prevented from getting near patients.

> Make sure you can explain the difference between antiseptic and aseptic surgery.

Joseph Lister

Lister introduced new ideas on cleanliness in surgery in the late 1800s leading to what some historians call the Revolution in Surgery. Before he introduced **sterile surgery** (surgery free from germs) many people died due to infection. After reading Pasteur's germ theory, Lister started to use carbolic acid to cover wounds and spray on instruments to keep them clean. He also insisted on hand-washing in surgery. His ideas were taken on by many surgeons and infection rates dropped greatly as a result. This showed that germ theory was correct and that patients' lives could be saved with attention to cleanliness, something other reformers such as Semmelweis and Nightingale had long been campaigning for.

War

- War played a big part in getting anaesthetics, antiseptics and aseptic surgery accepted.
- Battlefield surgeons used all of these techniques with success in the Crimean War and later during the First World War, showing sceptical doctors and surgeons that the techniques were valid and could reduce the loss of patients through pain and infection.

> War is one of the factors you will need to be able to talk about.

> For more on Pasteur, turn to pages 14 and 16.

> For more on anaesthetics, turn to page 19.

Now try this

Explain why the work of Lister was so important in persuading people that germ theory was correct.

Industrial Britain

As a result of the Industrial Revolution (1780–1850) people in towns lived close together in poor conditions. This led to terrible public health problems. During the 19th century, theories on causes and treatment of disease began to change and great improvements were made to public health.

Impact of the Industrial Revolution

The Industrial Revolution meant many changes.

- The population grew and after 1850 there were more people living in towns than in the countryside for the first time.
- Most working people were employed in the new industrial jobs rather than in agriculture.
- Wages were low and hours were very long.
- Children as well as adults worked in dangerous conditions with frequent accidents.

Theories about the causes of disease

- Most of the ideas about the causes of disease that had been around since medieval times were still in place. By the 19th century the most widely believed theory about the cause of disease was still miasma.
- The first public health measures were based on miasma and though the idea was wrong, the measures had some effect because they focused on making towns cleaner.

Epidemics

In the 1820s, 1830s and 1840s there were frequent and deadly waves of epidemic disease including:

- influenza
- cholera
- typhus
- typhoid
- smallpox.

You can read more about smallpox on page 13. You can find out more about cholera on page 22.

'A Court for King Cholera': a cartoon from 1852 linking cholera to the filthy conditions people lived in.

Medieval public health

- ✓ A lot of people lived so close together that diseases spread very quickly.
- ✓ There were no sewers and no rules for getting rid of waste.
- ✓ Most people would get their water from streams and rivers, which were often **contaminated** (polluted) with human waste.
- ✓ Butchers would slaughter their animals in the streets and leave the waste.
- ✓ Towns were usually so dirty that they smelled very bad.
- ✓ Some councils did try to clean up towns.

19th century public health

- ✓ Most towns were very overcrowded with many poor quality houses crammed into a small area.
- ✓ Pay was low so poverty was widespread.
- ✓ There were very often no systems or rules for getting rid of waste: it was left in the streets and got into the water supply.
- ✓ Clean water was in very short supply.
- ✓ Outbreaks of diseases such as cholera and typhus were frequent and deadly.
- ✓ Different groups argued about whether the government should interfere or not. Mostly the government took a **laissez-faire** (leave it alone) attitude.
- ✓ In 1848 a terrible cholera epidemic scared the government into action with the first public health measures.

For more about public health in the Middle Ages, turn to pages 7–8.

You will need to be able to **compare** features like public health across two different time periods for Question 3 on the exam paper.

For more about the 1848 Public Health Act, turn to page 23.

Now try this

Write **three** sentences to show similarities between public health in Medieval Britain and in 19th century Britain.

Public health reformers

As the 19th century progressed, public health in industrial Britain was completely transformed by the work of public health reformers and, eventually, the government.

Cholera as an agent of change

- **Cholera** arrived in Britain in 1831. The symptoms were horrific and the disease spread through cramped and dirty towns at an alarming pace, killing both rich and poor.
- The cholera outbreak of 1848 was worse than any other and became an **agent of change** as people demanded something be done, forcing the government to act.
- After this the government introduced Public Health Acts to improve living conditions and people's health.

For more on government involvement in public health, turn to page 23.

What is cholera?

Cholera is an infectious disease that can kill very quickly if it isn't treated. It is caused by eating contaminated food or drinking contaminated water. Not everyone infected with the bacterium – which is called *Vibrio cholerae* – develops symptoms. However, symptoms can be nasty and include severe diarrhoea and dehydration.

John Snow

Snow was a leading doctor in Victorian Britain. He worked out that the 1854 cholera outbreak in London was caused by contaminated water by recording deaths from the disease and showing they were centred around one particular water pump. He took the handle off the pump and the number of deaths fell. Later scientists realised this was early proof of germ theory.

For more on germ theory, see pages 14–18.

Joseph Bazalgette

The Great Stink of 1858 was a very hot summer in which the heat made the smell of untreated human waste in the River Thames unbearable. This, along with frequent and deadly cholera outbreaks, meant the problem of how to get rid of all waste in London could no longer be ignored. Bazalgette engineered a huge, complex and expensive network of sewers to move waste through massive pipes under the city and out to the tidal parts of the River Thames, where it would be swept out to sea.

Bazalgette's work is a great example of the impact of technology on public health.

Edwin Chadwick

Chadwick investigated the living conditions of the poor. After outbreaks of **influenza**, **typhoid** and **cholera** the government asked Chadwick to write a report about living conditions.
He was able to show a direct link between poor living conditions and disease. The government could not ignore this and his findings inspired the **1848 Public Health Act**.

For more about the Public Health Acts of 1848 and 1875, turn to page 23.

William Farr

Farr pioneered the idea of medical statistics. He set up a system of recording the causes of deaths, which meant people could better understand the public health problems that led to people dying. His statistics were vital in helping Snow to prove that cholera came from water.

Now try this

Choose **one** of the reformers above. Write **two** sentences explaining why his work was important.

Government involvement

During the 1800s the government had to abandon its laissez-faire attitude to public health and introduced a series of Public Health Acts and interventions.

Reasons for change

Before the 1840s the government's policy was not to interfere in situations, so that people would learn to help themselves (the laissez-faire approach). There was a number of reasons why this slowly changed:

- Epidemics – people demanded action following a deadly cholera outbreak in 1847.
- Extension of the franchise – more people voting meant more people to put pressure on the government.
- The work of individual reformers such as Farr, Snow, Chadwick and Bazalgette.

Remember, the government was scared into this Act by yet another terrible cholera outbreak.

1848 Public Health Act

- This was the first real Public Health Act, and the first time the government had really changed its policy of the laissez-faire approach.
- It created a Central Board of Health and **encouraged** setting up of local Boards of Health.
- These were **supposed** to appoint a medical officer, to provide sewers, inspect houses and check that food offered for sale was actually fit for humans.

It is a good idea to know how the Acts can be divided up in case you are asked to write about them in depth.

Types of government involvement

The government got involved in public health in a number of areas:

- ✓ Housing
- ✓ Working conditions
- ✓ Medical care
- ✓ Sanitation.

You can also divide the Acts into categories according to how they were enforced:

- ✓ Mandatory/compulsory (forcing people to act)
- ✓ National Standards (encouraging people to act)
- ✓ Reinforcing (backing up an Act that hadn't previously worked).

1875 Public Health Act

- This was actually the bringing together of a number of Acts covering clean water, improvements to housing and control of disease.
- The local authorities now **had** to appoint medical officers to oversee public health. Local inspectors were supposed to inspect abattoirs and stop contaminated food from getting into the food chain.
- Local authorities were now **required** to arrange for sewers to be maintained and to supply fresh water and rubbish collections.

Timeline

Other government involvement

1853 Compulsory Vaccination – vaccination against smallpox was made mandatory (although no one was given the authority to enforce this).

1864 Factory Act – aimed at improving conditions in factories (National Standard).

1871 Vaccination Act – aimed at backing up the previous Act in 1853 (Reinforcing).

1834 Poor Law Amendment Act – appointing medical officers to provide basic medical care for the very poor (National Standard).

1855 Nuisance Removal Act – trying to make overcrowded housing illegal (National Standard).

1866 Sanitary Act – forcing local authorities to take responsibility for sewerage and providing clean water (National Standard).

Now try this

Give **three** reasons why the government had to change its policy of laissez-faire.

Developments in drugs

At the beginning of the 20th century the focus was still on **treating** diseases because doctors could do little to actually **cure** them. This changed with the discovery of **penicillin** and its development by the **pharmaceutical industry**.

Penicillin

The **pharmaceutical industry** researches, produces and sells medicines.

1928 Tidying his lab, **Alexander Fleming** finds a Petri dish with mould growing on it and realises that the mould has killed some of the bacteria around it. He works out which bacteria the **penicillin** mould can kill. Fleming writes about this discovery in a medical journal.

↓

1938 Scientists **Howard Florey** and **Ernst Chain** discover a method of purifying and producing penicillin.

↓

1940 Florey and Chain use mice to test penicillin. The **Second World War** means there isn't enough money for British companies to produce the drug.

↓

1941 Florey and Chain turn their lab at Oxford University into a penicillin factory; trials have positive results. Florey seeks assistance in the US. The US government sees its potential and offers funding.

↓

1943 Florey trials the drug, using small doses to treat soldiers' war wounds in North Africa. Many lives are saved. Mass-production begins in Britain.

↓

1945 Margaret Hutchinson **Rousseau** develops a mass-production method. This produces 650 billion doses in 1945.

Factors in the development of penicillin

- War (The US government saw the potential of penicillin for treating their injured soldiers.)
- Chance (Fleming saw the penicillin mould by chance.)
- Government (The US government funded Florey and Chain's research.)
- Science and technology (Hutchinson Rousseau's method meant penicillin could be mass-produced.)
- The role of the individual (Without the vital work of Florey and Chain, penicillin might not have been developed for years.)

You can use penicillin to highlight some of the **factors** you need to know about. Remember, more than one factor can be important in a big development in medicine.

Drug development

- Before penicillin, drugs had been researched, tested and even manufactured, but not on such a large scale.
- After the Second World War a large pharmaceutical industry grew. Today the industry researches, develops, tests and produces many types of drugs.
- Drug companies are still looking for cures for illnesses like cancer, **AIDS** or the common cold.
- The cost of research and development of drugs is very high but drug companies often make large profits on selling drugs that they have developed.

Drug safety

- Drug development hasn't always been a success. Until the 1960s every new drug was seen as a positive discovery until the **thalidomide** disaster, when a drug aimed at helping pregnant women with morning sickness caused babies to be born with malformed limbs.
- Thalidomide led to much stricter controls on drug testing and approval in countries including Britain. The drug is used today to treat AIDS and **leprosy** but it is still controversial.

Now try this

Write a paragraph explaining the roles of chance and war in the development of penicillin.

New diseases and treatments

New treatments for some diseases have emerged as a result of developments in science and technology. Being better at finding treatments is not without its problems and antibiotic resistance provides one of the greatest challenges to modern medicine. Some people prefer to use **alternative medicines** to treat illness.

Antibiotic resistance

An **antibiotic** is a medicine used to kill microorganisms and treat infectious diseases. Penicillin is an example of an antibiotic.

- One of the greatest problems facing modern medicine is **antibiotic resistance** (also known as antimicrobial resistance or AMR).
- Over time, some of the bacteria that have been treated by the antibiotics developed since the discovery of **penicillin** have become resistant to these treatments. This is partly due to overuse of these antibiotics and partly due to people not completing their course of treatment.
- The World Health Organization (WHO) said in September 2016 that the danger to the world from antibiotic resistance was now so great that it was making fighting diseases such as TB, AIDS and malaria much harder and would soon make things like **chemotherapy** treatment for cancer too high risk.

You can find more about penicillin on page 24.

MRSA

One of the biggest problems in hospitals in Britain today is the 'superbug', MRSA. The infections caused by MRSA can be life-threatening.

A **superbug** is a type of bacteria that is resistant to most antibiotics, making it difficult to treat.

The NHS promotes hand hygiene, reminding patients of the importance of clean hands in the fight against infection and encouraging them to ask medical staff if they have washed their hands. Thanks to strict hand-washing and cleanliness, the rates of MRSA infections in British hospitals have dropped.

HIV and AIDS

AIDS is a recently recognised disease caused by the HIV virus. HIV attacks the immune system, and weakens the body's ability to fight infections and disease. It was first discovered in 1981 but it wasn't until 1983 that scientists worked out that it was a viral infection. Like most viral infections there is no cure for HIV, but treatments have been developed to allow most people with HIV to live a normal life for many years after diagnosis. AIDS is the last stage of the HIV infection, when the body has no resistance to simple infections.

Alternative medicine and treatments

Alternative treatments use approaches that may not be scientifically proven, but many people find them effective. They include:

- ☑ acuncture (inserting fine needles into the skin with the aim of assisting the body to balance itself)
- ☑ hypnotherapy (using hypnosis as a treatment for illness)
- ☑ herbal medicines ('natural' medicines made from plants, trees or fungi).

You'll need to be able to **compare** treatments across different periods for Question 3 in the exam and say what is similar and different about them. For example you might be asked to compare quackery in the Renaissance with alternative medicine today.

Turn to page 10 for more on quackery.

Now try this

Give **two** similarities between hospitals in the late 18th/early 19th centuries and the modern fight against MRSA.

Use the information on page 12 about hospitals in the 18th and 19th centuries to help you.

Developments in surgery

The 20th century saw some of the biggest changes to surgery, with the introduction of plastic surgery, blood transfusions, X-rays and transplant surgery.

X-rays were discovered by Wilhelm Roentgen in 1895 and **radiation therapy** using X-ray machines was used for treating cancer by 1901. X-rays for diagnosis became popular with military doctors during the First World War, and both X-rays and radiation therapy became widespread in hospitals in the 1930s. They are now routinely used for diagnosis and for cancer treatment.

Blood transfusion (taking blood from one person and injecting it into another) had been attempted in the 1600s but in 1901 Karl Landsteiner identified blood groups, paving the way for work on blood transfusions.

Major developments in surgery

Plastic surgery was first used by Archibald McIndoe to rebuild the faces of airmen burned in the Second World War.

Techniques in keyhole surgery (entering the body through a tiny hole) and **laser surgery** (using lasers during surgery to treat conditions) have developed and are now mainstream in most British hospitals.

Open-heart surgery was performed first in 1950 by Wilfred G. Bigelow.

The first kidney **transplants** took place in America in 1954, and in 1967 South African surgeon Christiaan Barnard performed the first successful heart transplant. In 1970 the drug **cyclosporine** was developed to stop the body rejecting transplanted organs.

War and surgery

- War in the 20th century involved much bigger weapons, which did much more damage, requiring the development of new techniques.
- The First World War had a particularly big impact on surgery. There were new developments in **orthopaedic surgery** and **neurosurgery** on the battlefield which were later used to treat civilians.
- Developments during the First and Second World Wars made blood transfusions widespread.

Orthopaedic surgery deals with damaged bones or muscles. **Neurosurgery** deals with damage to the nervous system, including the brain.

Surgery is performed on a wounded soldier at a Mobile Army Surgical Hospital (MASH) during the Korean War. MASH units were set up close to the front so that soldiers could be treated much more quickly.

During the First World War surgeon Geoffrey Keynes developed a machine to store blood and carry out transfusions.

By the Second World War refrigeration technology meant blood banks could be set up.

Technology and surgery

X-ray machines are used to work out what is wrong with a patient before performing surgery and during surgery to make sure it has been successful.

Since 1945 billions of deaths during surgery from infection have been prevented using penicillin. Penicillin was able to be mass-produced thanks to technology engineered by Margaret Hutchinson Rousseau in 1945.

Now try this

Use the information on this page and page 24 to write a paragraph explaining how war was important in the development of surgery in the 20th century.

Liberal social reforms

In the late 19th and early 20th centuries the government accepted that they needed to have a much bigger role in helping people, thanks to the work of individuals like **Booth** and **Rowntree**, which the new Liberal Government was keen to take on.

Charles Booth

Booth was a wealthy businessman and social researcher who produced a report on poverty among the working classes of London in 1892, called *Life and Labour of the People in London*. Unlike writers of earlier reports, he had actually spent time with the poor and medical professionals in the area and concluded that 30% of London lived in poverty. Importantly, his report challenged the idea that the poor were to blame for their situation.

Seebohm Rowntree

Between 1899 and 1901 Rowntree worked with Booth on a study of poverty in York called *Poverty, A Study of Town Life*. Together they used statistics to prove that poverty was not unique to London but widespread across the country. They showed that 30% of York lived in poverty too. He came up with the term **'poverty line'** to describe the amount of money people had to earn to simply stay out of poverty. Like Booth's *London* report, it stressed that people couldn't help being poor.

The Second Boer War

- The **Second Boer War** in South Africa lasted from 1899 to 1902 and a lot of young British men volunteered to fight.

- However, many of these men didn't pass the medical tests and around a third of all recruits weren't healthy enough.

- There were worries that if Britain was involved in a bigger war, there would not be enough men who were fit enough to fight. The government had to do something.

The National Insurance Act, 1911

- National Health Insurance was given to workers earning less than £160 per year, funded by workers, employers and the government all putting money in.

- National Health Insurance gave people sickness benefit, maternity benefits and free medical treatment (up to a limit).

- Unemployment benefit was given to workers in some trades who lost their job, funded by a contribution from the worker and from the government.

The Liberal Government, 1906–1914

At the beginning of the 20th century some people were still struggling with terrible poverty. The only help they would get was from charities like **Barnardo's** or the **Salvation Army**. The Liberal Government decided it had to do more to help people. The Boer Wars and worries about the efficiency of the workforce led to the introduction of a number of new social reforms:

- **Children's charter**: In **1906** the government introduced school meals and in **1907** introduced medical inspections in schools.

- **Old-age pensions**: In **1908** the Liberal Government brought in pensions, which paid 25 pence a week to people over 70 living below the poverty line unless they hadn't worked or had been in prison.

- **Health and Unemployment Insurance**: Poor people still struggled to pay for medical treatment and those out of work often lived in extreme poverty. **The National Insurance Act, 1911** tried to do something about this.

These measures weren't entirely successful and by the time of the First World War poverty, and the ill-health and diseases related to it, was still a problem.

Now try this

Write **three** sentences explaining why the Second Boer War led to government reforms in public health.

Impact of war

The two World Wars in the first half of the 20th century had a huge impact on public health. Changes were made to housing and the government introduced new measures to tackle poverty, which was still a problem.

The First World War

- Despite the efforts made by the government after the Second Boer War, many young men signing up for the First World War were too unhealthy to serve.

- The country wanted its heroes from the war to come back to a better life.

- The First World War was supposed to be the 'war to end all wars'. The experience of the war was terrible for many people. The government had to act to improve public health.

Turn to page 29 for more on the Beveridge Report and its consequences.

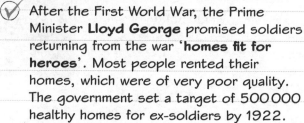

Homes fit for heroes

✓ After the First World War, the Prime Minister **Lloyd George** promised soldiers returning from the war '**homes fit for heroes**'. Most people rented their homes, which were of very poor quality. The government set a target of 500 000 healthy homes for ex-soldiers by 1922.

✓ During the Second World War the government had to rebuild areas which had been damaged by bombing and also deal with the problems in housing identified by the **Beveridge Report** so again decided to build lots of houses: this was the beginning of **council housing**.

Interwar health measures

✓ Between the World Wars some big changes were made to public health.

✓ Changes were made to the training of doctors and nurses, and hospitals were reorganised to become better value for money.

✓ The **Ministry of Health** was created in 1919, run by a minister who had been a doctor.

✓ Local authorities had to set up special hospitals called **sanatoria** to look after people with **tuberculosis**.

✓ In **1934** the **Free School Milk Act** gave free milk to children in schools every day.

Impact of the two World Wars on poverty

The **First World War** had a big impact on poverty and greatly improved the lives of many of the nation's poorest citizens. It also saw changes to the status of women who had to work to help the war effort – they could work more easily after the war too, reducing poverty.

The **Second World War** led to the Beveridge Report and eventually to the creation of the **Welfare State**, which was supposed to end poverty in Britain. It was not entirely successful but it did reduce poverty and its associated problems.

Turn to page 29 for more on the Welfare State.

The Second World War

- During the war the country was run by a **coalition government** made up of Labour, Conservative and Liberal politicians.

- People faced many challenges, including **bombing**, **rationing** and **evacuation**.

- In these hard times the government organised many aspects of daily life and the public welcomed this.

- These challenges of the Second World War led to the Beveridge Report.

Soldiers in a military hospital in France, 1940, receiving a daily ration of wine. Diet and healthcare for soldiers were often better than on the **Home Front** and during peacetime.

Now try this

List **two** reasons why the First World War led to better housing for people in Britain.

The Welfare State and the NHS

The Beveridge Report, 1942, led to the creation of the Welfare State, with the intention that no one would ever again have to live in poverty. Part of this was the setting up of the NHS, which aimed to provide everyone with free healthcare when they needed it. The NHS wasn't popular with everyone.

The Beveridge Report

- **William Beveridge** was the expert appointed to lead a committee looking into **social security** in Britain during the Second World War. He had been involved in the Liberal Government and helped it come up with its social policies and reforms.
- The committee decided there were five main problems with British society that stopped people making a better life for themselves. These were known as the Five Giants.
- The *Report on Social Insurance and Allied Services* was published in December 1942 and quickly became known as the **Beveridge Report**.

Social security is financial assistance from the state for people with low or no income.

Recommendations of the report

The report said that Britain needed a proper system for welfare which would be:

- available to all **at the point of need**
- **non-means tested** – even if people couldn't afford to pay they would still get help
- **comprehensive** – covering all of the problems poverty caused
- **contributory** – paid for by people in their wages
- **compulsory** – everyone paying into the system.

The system that would provide social security for all became known as the **Welfare State** and still exists today.

For more about the Liberal Government and social reforms, turn to page 27.

Ignorance (from a lack of quality education)

Want (caused by poverty)

Squalor (caused by poor housing conditions)

The Five Giants

Idleness (from unemployment)

Disease (caused by a poor quality health system)

The NHS

- In 1948 the **NHS (National Health Service)** was set up by **Aneurin Bevan** as part of the Welfare State.
- People had had free healthcare during the war and wanted it to continue.
- In the first year the service was very popular and great improvements were made in public health.
- New hospitals followed as part of the plans and the rate of many killer diseases began to fall for the first time.

Opposition to the NHS

Not everyone was convinced the NHS was a good idea. A lot of doctors disliked it as they wanted the right to keep charging patients for treating them privately, rather than being employed by the government.

You can find out about the successes and failures of the NHS, as well as its challenges in the 21st century, on page 30.

Now try this

Write **two** sentences explaining why doctors were against the NHS.

Had a look ☐   Nearly there ☐   Nailed it! ☐

Healthcare in the 21st century

The NHS was seen as the greatest achievement of the Welfare State. It has helped many people. However, it almost immediately ran into problems that continue to this day.

Early successes and challenges for the NHS

Successes	Challenges
👍 Improvement to maternity services and services for children reduced illness and death among babies and children by a huge amount.	👎 The plan to pay for the NHS out of National Insurance contributions didn't work, as it only covered 10 per cent of the cost.
👍 New hospitals were built with modern equipment and much better treatment facilities.	👎 Hospitals were not able to care for the number of people who came forward for treatment. Bevan had got doctors to agree to the NHS by promising them new hospitals. This was very expensive and many hospitals took a long time to build, leaving the system struggling.
👍 Education campaigns designed to prevent illness rather than treat it had great success.	👎 The cost of the new system was so high that by the 1950s changes had to be made, such as introducing prescription charges and rethinking what treatments were free.
👍 The NHS vaccination campaign got rid of some of the most deadly diseases, such as polio and tuberculosis.	

A lot of these challenges continue to this day.

How does the NHS pay for everything it needs to as the population grows?

Which treatments should the NHS pay for?

COST

How do we pay for hospitals, which are expensive to build and run?

Should everything still be free?

Litigation means taking legal action – taking someone to court.

Questions facing the NHS today

What illnesses should the NHS treat?

Should illnesses that are often self-inflicted (such as those caused by smoking) be treated for free?

ETHICS ⬅ Ethics involves decisions about right and wrong.

Should people be made to change their lifestyle before getting treatment?

LITIGATION

Should people be allowed to sue the NHS when treatment goes wrong?

How can the NHS pay for legal action brought against it?

EFFECTIVENESS

Should there be targets for the NHS to meet?

The **pharmaceutical industry** makes very big profits. Sometimes drugs are so expensive that the NHS cannot afford them and people can only access them privately, by paying a lot of money.

Now try this

Name **three** challenges facing the NHS today that are the same as in the early days of the NHS.

Exam overview

This page introduces you to the main features and requirements of the Paper 2 Section A exam paper for Option 2A.

About Paper 2

- Paper 2 is for your thematic study and your British depth study.

- Section A of the paper will be on your thematic study, which is Britain: Health and the people: c1000 to the present day.

- You must answer **all** questions in Section A.

- You will receive two documents: a question paper which will contain the questions and a source, and an answer booklet.

> The Paper 2 exam lasts for 1 hour 45 minutes (105 minutes). There are 84 marks in total: **40 marks, plus 4 marks for spelling, punctuation and grammar, for Section A;** 40 marks for Section B. You should spend approximately **50 minutes on Section A** and 50 minutes on Section B, with 5 minutes to check your answers.

> Here we are focusing on Section A and your Option 2A thematic study. However, the same exam paper will also include Section B, where you will answer questions about your British depth study.

The questions

The questions for Paper 2 Section A will always follow this pattern.

> You can see examples of all four questions on pages 35–38 and in the practice questions on pages 41–47.

Question 1
Study **Source A**.
How useful is **Source A** to an historian studying …?
Explain your answer using **Source A** and your contextual knowledge.　　**(8 marks)**

> Question 1 targets AO3. AO3 is about analysing, evaluating and making judgements about sources. Spend about 10 minutes on this question, which asks you to **evaluate the usefulness of a source**.

Question 2
Explain the significance of …　　**(8 marks)**

> Question 2 targets both AO1 and AO2. AO1 is about showing your knowledge and understanding of the **key features and characteristics** of the topic. AO2 is about explaining and analysing historical events using **historical concepts**, such as causation, consequence, change, continuity, similarity and difference. Spend about 10 minutes on this question, which focuses on **explaining the significance** of a key event, development or individual over time.

Question 3
Compare …
In what ways were they similar/different?
Explain your answer with reference to both …
　　(8 marks)

> Question 3 also targets AO1 and AO2. Spend about 10 minutes on this question, which asks you to **compare** similarity or difference.

Question 4
Has … been the main factor in …?
Explain your answer with reference to … and other factors.　　**(16 marks + 4 marks for SPaG)**

> Question 4 also targets AO1 and AO2. Spend about 20 minutes on this essay question, which asks you to **evaluate** one factor against other factors. You will need to make a **judgement** in your answer to this question. Up to 4 marks are available for **spelling, punctuation** and **grammar** (SPaG).

Source skills 1

Question 1 is based on **one source**. The question will ask you about the **usefulness** of this source to an historian studying a particular enquiry.

What is a source?

A source is a piece of evidence that comes from the time period or event it describes. There are various types of source. In the exam you will be given only one source, but it could be either **a visual one or a written one** – so make sure you are prepared for both.

What is contextual knowledge?

Question 1 will ask you to explain your answer using the source and your **contextual knowledge**. You will need to think about what you know about the topic in the question and how the source fits with what you know. Only use knowledge that is **relevant** to the topic and that is linked to the source itself.

Examples of visual sources

Visual sources include:

- Posters
- Adverts
- Photographs
- Drawings or cartoons
- Paintings
- Plans of buildings

Examples of written sources

Written sources include:

- Speeches
- Letters
- Extracts from books
- Extracts from diaries
- Newspaper reports
- Government reports

Hints and tips on usefulness

To answer question 1 you will need to **evaluate** the usefulness of the source you are given. This means you will need to explain your ideas about how useful the source is to the enquiry given in the question. You will then need to come to a **judgement** about useful it is. To evaluate the source, you need to consider three things: **content**, **provenance** and **contextual knowledge**.

1 Content

- What information in the source is relevant to the enquiry?
- How useful is this information?
- Are there ways that the source isn't useful?

Spend some time underlining and annotating information in the source to help you.

Remember: this isn't about the amount of information given – a small piece of information can still be useful.

It's always good to give a balanced answer if you can, but remember to focus on how it **is** useful.

2 Provenance

- Nature: the type of source it is.
- Origin: who produced it and when.
- Purpose: why the source was created.

How do these things affect the usefulness of the source? Remember: an unreliable source can still be useful.

3 Contextual knowledge

- Use your own relevant knowledge of the enquiry topic to **evaluate** the source.
- Does the source back up what you know about the enquiry?
- Is all of the information in the source accurate compared with what you know?

Remember: you need to think about what information is missing from the source as well as what's included.

When you use your own knowledge, make sure you say clearly how it relates to the source.

Source skills 2

It's important you spend time reading and looking at the source carefully before you start your answer to question 1. You could underline and make notes on the source to help you.

Source A Aspects of the Great Plague of London, 1665, shown in a newspaper of the time. The top image shows the people fleeing; the bottom image shows the dead being buried in mass graves.

You will be given short details to help you understand what is in the source. You can use this to inform your answer. This is where you can find out about the **provenance** (nature, origin and purpose) of the source.

Take notice of any dates given. Think about what you know was happening at this time in relation to the enquiry.

Visual sources need as much analysing as written ones. What can you see in the image? What can't you see? How useful is this to the enquiry?

Source A Extract from the diary of Samuel Pepys, a London resident famous for writing a diary. These extracts were written over the first months in 1665 that the plague hit London.

How well qualified is this person to give information relevant to your enquiry? This will affect how useful any information given is.

Remember to take notice of any dates given. Think about what you know was happening at this time in relation to the enquiry.

> **30th April 1665**
> Great fears of the sickness here in the City, it being said that two or three houses are already shut up. God preserve us all.
>
> **7th June 1665**
> This day, much against my Will, I did in Drury-lane see two or three houses marked with a red cross upon the doors, and 'Lord have mercy upon us' writ there – which was a sad sight to me … I was forced to buy some roll tobacco to smell to.
>
> **31st August 1665**
> Every day sadder and sadder news of its increase. In the City died this week 7496; and all of them, 6102 of the plague. But it is feared that the true number of the dead this week is near 10 000 – partly from the poor that cannot be taken notice of through the greatness of the number.

When you read through the source, highlight any information which is directly relevant to the enquiry.

Source A

This source is referred to in the worked example on page 35.

SECTION A

Britain: Health and the people

Source A for use in answering question **1** on page 35.

Source A   The front cover of the popular Victorian Magazine *The Million* from 1894. The picture is entitled 'The Travelling Quack' and shows a patent medicine salesman.

Question 1: evaluating usefulness

Question 1 on your exam paper will ask you to study Source A and explain how useful it is to an historian studying a development in medicine and public health.

Worked example

Study **Source A** on page 34.

How useful is **Source A** to an historian studying quackery?

Explain your answer using **Source A** and your contextual knowledge.   **(8 marks)**

Sample extract

Source A shows a patent medicine salesman or 'quack' in 1894. This source is useful for this enquiry because it shows a salesman selling patent medicines which were medicines with no real scientific background that often did nothing at all. Sometimes, though, they contained harmful substances like cocaine or mercury. It comes from a very popular Victorian magazine which suggests that it can be trusted as a record of what was going on at the time.

The picture is useful as it seems to show a travelling salesman, confirming for us that this was how quack doctors usually operated. By the time their patients worked out the medicine didn't do what it claimed it did, the salesman would have moved on to a different location.

Quack medicine was very popular in medieval times but the source shows us that it is still being practised in Victorian times when ideas about disease had supposedly changed. We know this because the source is from a very popular Victorian magazine. This is useful as it shows that even in 1894 people were sceptical about germ theory and scientific ideas about what caused disease.

It is also useful because it shows that some people obviously didn't have access to the kinds of doctors who would practise the more scientific ideas and these people still had to resort to quacks.

The source doesn't, however, show us how widespread quack medicine was by this time and as we can't see the article that the cover relates to. It may be that it is talking about how it isn't that popular any more now the new ideas are being accepted.

 Links   You can revise quackery on page 10.

What do 'explain' and 'how useful' mean?

Explain means to set your ideas out in detail — in this case 'how useful' a source is to an historian.

How useful means how valuable the source is for a specific enquiry – you need to come to a judgement on how useful the source is for the enquiry given in the question.

Make sure you get straight to answering the question by saying **how** the source is useful for the specific enquiry.

Paragraph 1 is good because the student starts to bring in some of their **own knowledge** to contextualise the source. It also talks about **provenance** (where the source comes from) and how this can make it useful.

Stick tightly to the question by repeating that the source is useful, then give another reason why.

By comparing the time period in the source with another time period you can show you understand the **historical context**.

You can also talk about how the source is limited in its usefulness like this student does; this shows a deep understanding of usefulness.

Make sure all of the information in your answer is **relevant**.

Question 2: explaining significance

Question 2 is an 'explaining significance' question. You will be asked to explain the **significance** of a key event, development or individual over time. You will also need to consider **historical concepts**.

For a reminder about historical concepts, turn to page 31.

Worked example

Explain the significance of vaccination in the health of the people since 1000.   **(8 marks)**

 Links You can revise vaccination on pages 13 and 16.

Sample extract

Vaccination has been very significant in the development of medicine for a number of reasons.

Without vaccination many diseases that caused huge numbers of deaths would still be prevalent in our world. A good example of this is smallpox. Before Jenner's discovery of the smallpox vaccine the disease could kill thousands of people in one outbreak. An outbreak in 1796 killed about 34 000 people. Thanks to Jenner's discovery, though, by 1980 smallpox had been eradicated from the world through large-scale programmes of vaccination worldwide.

Another reason vaccination is so significant is that it shows the importance of individuals in improving the health of people. If it hadn't been for Jenner's genius ideas and Pasteur's conviction that germ theory could help him to produce vaccinations in the lab, which could then be mass-produced, the idea might not have gone anywhere.

Vaccination also shows that the discovery of the idea of vaccination wasn't as significant as the development of it. Science and technology meant that vaccines could be developed in the lab and mass-produced, while finance from drug companies and government funding meant that programmes of vaccination could be rolled out and eventually kill off horrible diseases like smallpox.

What is 'significance'?

Significance looks at the importance of a key event, person/group or development at the time and importance over time. In this example you are asked to explain the significance of vaccination.

Remember to stick closely to the question and get straight to the point.

You need to include **specific knowledge** about vaccination, with as much **detail** as you can.

Make sure you give **more than one reason** why something – in this case, vaccination – is significant, and be sure to include details to back up your ideas.

Try to explore the **relationship** between aspects of significance, as this student does. The best answers do this.

Question 3: making comparisons

Question 3 is a 'compare' question. You will be asked to show your understanding of **similarity** or **difference**. You will also need to consider **historical concepts**.

For a reminder about historical concepts, turn to page 31.

Worked example

Compare hospitals in the medieval period with hospitals in the late 18th and early 19th centuries.

In what ways were they similar?

Explain your answer with reference to both periods.

(8 marks)

🔗 **Links**   You can revise medieval hospitals on page 4 and hospitals in 1800 on page 12.

What does 'compare' mean?

Compare means to identify **similarities or differences** between things. In this example it's similarities between hospitals in the medieval period and hospitals in the late 18th/early 19th centuries.

Sample extract

Hospitals in the medieval period were mainly run by the Church and by monks and nuns from the nearby religious houses. In 1800 this wasn't the case anymore and most hospitals were not set up by or controlled by the Church.

Medieval hospitals weren't all about hospitality and religious pilgrims. Some of them specialised in certain illnesses, such as Bedlam, which focused on people with mental illnesses.

Also, some early hospitals were centres for the training of doctors and nurses in the same way hospitals in 1800 were after the work of people like Hunter and Nightingale.

Another example of how they were similar is cleanliness and hygiene. Florence Nightingale made great improvements in this area with her books *Notes on Nursing* and *Notes on Hospitals*, but medieval hospitals were often kept very clean by monks and nuns who understood the importance of being clean for health even if they did not know the science behind it.

This is a great way to start. Don't waste time on a lengthy introduction, just get straight to answering the question.

Remember that even though the question says 'Compare', the focus in this example is on 'In what ways were they **similar**?'. The question will make it clear whether you need to talk about similarities **or** differences.

Make sure you show your knowledge by including plenty of accurate details, as this student does. The best answers do this.

You should compare **more than one** similarity (or difference, if the focus of the question is on difference) in your answer. Using words like 'also', as this student has done, helps to show you are doing this.

Make sure that your answer refers to **both** time periods.

Question 4: making a judgement 1

Question 4 asks you to **evaluate** factors and come to a **sustained judgement**.

Compare this answer with an improved version on the next page.

Worked example

Have individuals been the main factor in the development of medicine in Britain since medieval times?

Explain your answer with reference to individuals and other factors.

Use examples from your study of Health and the people.

(16 marks + 4 marks for SPaG)

Sample extract

Since medieval times individuals have been the most important factor because without individuals like Pasteur and Nightingale, medicine would still be like it was in medieval times.

Fleming invented penicillin, which is one of the most important drugs ever to be discovered, and Pasteur challenged ideas which came before him and showed what really caused disease, which is possibly the most important development in medicine ever. This meant that other scientists could come along later and use their ideas to improve medicine.

There are lots of key individuals in medicine who have probably been forgotten about and who will also have made a very important contribution.

Also, individuals have built on the work of each other since medieval times. For example, the work of Landsteiner on blood groups allowed people to better understand what Harvey was trying to say about circulation of blood 400 years earlier. Individuals have worked together (even if they lived a long time apart) to move medicine forward.

In conclusion, I believe individuals have been the most important factor in medicine since medieval times as without them big discoveries would not have been made and big improvements wouldn't have been introduced.

Links You will need all your knowledge of Health and the people since 1000 for this question, but you might want to revise key individuals such as:

Pasteur (pages 14 and 16); Koch (page 15); Ehrlich (page 17); Lister (page 20); Fleming, Florey and Chain (page 24).

Evaluating and making a judgement

This extended essay question will always pick one of the seven factors you have been studying: **war, superstition and religion, chance, government, communication, science and technology, the role of the individual**.

You need to **evaluate** the factor you are given against **other factors**: provide evidence, then make an informed **judgement** about it.

This is a good start because it gets straight to the point.

It is good to include some knowledge of your own, but you need to be more detailed than this. For example, here you could comment on how Pasteur and Nightingale moved things on from medieval times.

Remember that 4 marks are available for SPaG: make sure you spell specialist words like **penicillin** correctly.

This information isn't really relevant in any way and gets in the way of creating a **sustained line of reasoning** (sticking to the point all the way through your answer).

Make sure you show **specific** knowledge and understanding, like this, rather than just making general points like 'Landsteiner and Harvey were important'.

Make sure you refer to other factors as well as the factor in focus – here, the role of individuals. This answer does not do this but the best answers do.

Question 4: making a judgement 2

This page has an improved version of the answer to question 4 on the previous page.

Improved extract

Since medieval times individuals have been the most important factor because without individuals like Pasteur and Nightingale medicine would still be like it was in medieval times. Pasteur's germ theory completely changed the way people thought about the causes of disease; before him people believed disease was a punishment from God, caused by smell or an imbalance of the Four Humours. Nightingale changed the way hospitals ran from the medieval ideas of hospitality and charity by improving how nurses were trained and used in her book *Notes on Nursing* and improving the cleanliness and safety of hospitals in her book *Notes on Hospitals*.

Fleming is another good example of an individual very important to improving medicine from medieval times. Fleming invented penicillin which is one of the most important drugs ever to be discovered, which was then developed by other individuals such as Florey and Chain. Without penicillin many infections like syphilis might still be out of control. However, it is important to know that chance played an important role in Fleming discovering penicillin and is therefore another important factor.

Pasteur challenged ideas which came before him and showed what really caused disease, which is possibly the most important development in medicine ever. This meant that other scientists such as Koch and Ehrlich could come along later and use their ideas to improve medicine with things like 'magic bullets' to kill the microbes which caused specific diseases. Other individuals have also built on the work of each other since medieval times. For example, the work of Landsteiner on blood groups allowed people to better understand what Harvey was trying to say about circulation of blood 400 years earlier. Individuals have worked together (even if they lived a long time apart) to move medicine forward.

Other factors are very important too. War is an important factor. The Crusades allowed the work of Muslim doctors such as Ibn Sina and Rhazes to be taken back to Europe where they improved things like surgery. During the First World War many big ideas were discovered or tested, such as X-rays and blood transfusions, and without the Second World War there would probably have been no development of penicillin, which I have already mentioned as being one of the most important drugs ever.

In conclusion, I believe individuals have been the most important factor in medicine since medieval times as without them big discoveries would not have been made and big improvements wouldn't have been introduced. However, there are other factors which are important such as war, just not as important as individuals.

Include **relevant detailed information** to show clearly that you understand the question and are answering it.

A sustained line of reasoning

In your answer to question 4 you need to show that you can develop a **sustained line of reasoning**. This means you need to show you can stick to the point throughout your answer. Make sure you:

- ✓ keep your points **relevant** to the question
- ✓ back up your ideas with **examples**
- ✓ **structure** your answer **logically**.

Use a wide range of **specialist terms** appropriately.

You **must** talk about other factors in addition to the one focused on in the question, as the student does here. The best answers do this.

The more factors you talk about the better, but remember that your knowledge has to be specific and quite detailed, and time is short – so choose the other factors you mention with care.

This answer suggests that one factor has greater merit than others – this is good.

Remember there are 4 marks on offer for **SPaG** so take time to check your answer carefully.

Practice

You will need to refer to the source below in your answer to question 1 on page 41.

SECTION A

Britain: Health and the people

Answer **all four questions** on pages 41 to 47.

Source A for use in answering question **1** on page 41.

Source A   An extract from the 1875 Public Health Act. The Act was designed to bring together a number of previous Acts. This section refers to the responsibility of local authorities for sewers and sewerage.

| Sewage to be purified before being discharged into streams | **17.** Nothing in this Act shall authorise any local authority to make or use any sewer[1] drain or outfall for the purpose of conveying sewage or filthy water into any natural stream or watercourse, or into any canal pond or lake until such sewage or filthy water is freed from all the excrementitious[2] or other foul or noxious[3] matter such as would affect or deteriorate[4] the purity and quality of the water in such stream or watercourse or in such canal pond or lake. |

[1]**sewer**: underground pipe for carrying off waste water and human waste
[2]**excrementitious**: relating to cast-out waste material
[3]**noxious**: harmful, very unpleasant
[4]**deteriorate**: make worse

Practice

Put your skills and knowledge into practice with the following question. You will need to refer to Source A on page 40 in your answer.

1 Study **Source A**.

How useful is **Source A** to an historian studying government involvement in 19th century public health improvement?

Explain your answer using **Source A** and your contextual knowledge.

(8 marks)

Guided Source A is useful to the historian studying

government involvement in 19th century public health

improvement because it shows

....

....

....

....

....

....

....

....

....

....

....

....

....

....

....

....

....

....

....

....

....

....

....

You have 1 hour 45 minutes for the **whole** of Paper 1 which means you have **50 minutes for Section A**. You should use the time carefully to answer all the questions fully. In the exam, remember to leave 5 minutes or so to check your work when you've finished both Sections A and B.

Links You can revise government involvement in public health improvement on page 23.

Spend about 10 minutes on this answer. Remember you need to focus on **usefulness**.

Remember the key things to look at in the source: content, provenance and how it fits with your own knowledge.

41

Practice

Use this page to continue your answer to question 1.

....

....

....

....

....

....

....

....

....

....

....

....

....

....

Remember, **explain** means to set something out in detail. In this case 'how useful' a source is to an historian.

How useful means how valuable the source is for this specific enquiry.

Practice

Put your skills and knowledge into practice with the following question.

2 Explain the significance of magic bullets in the development of medicine.

(8 marks)

Guided Magic bullets were significant in the development ....

of medicine because ....

....

....

....

....

....

....

....

....

....

....

....

....

....

....

....

....

....

....

....

....

....

....

....

....

You should spend about 10 minutes on this answer.

Links You can revise magic bullets on page 17.

Remember **significance** looks at the importance of a key event, person/group or development at the time, as well as importance over time. In this question you are asked to explain the significance of magic bullets.

You need to include **specific knowledge** about magic bullets with as much **detail** as you can.

Remember to cover **more than one** aspect of significance.

Practice

Use this page to continue your answer to question 2.

....

....

....

....

....

....

....

....

....

....

....

....

Try to write about the **relationship** between different aspects of significance. The best answers do this.

Practice

Put your skills and knowledge into practice with the following question.

3　Compare public health in towns in the Middle Ages with towns in 1875.

In what ways were they similar?

Explain your answer with reference to both times.

(8 marks)

Guided　Towns in the Middle Ages were not particularly

clean, however

....

....

....

....

....

....

....

....

....

....

....

....

....

....

....

....

....

....

....

....

....

....

....

....

You should spend about 10 minutes on this answer.

Links　You can revise public health in medieval towns on page 7, and public health improvements leading up to 1875 on pages 21–23.

Remember this question asks for **how they were similar** not a general comparison. The question will always make it clear whether it wants you to talk about similarities **or** differences.

Make sure you show your knowledge by including plenty of accurate **details**. The best answers do this.

You should compare **more than one** similarity in your answer. Using words like 'also' helps to show you are doing this.

45

Practice

Use this page to continue your answer to question 3.

....

....

....

....

....

....

....

....

....

....

....

....

....

Make sure your answer refers to **both** time periods.

Practice

Put your skills and knowledge into practice with the following question.

4 Has war been the main factor in the development of medicine and public health in Britain since medieval times? Explain your answer with reference to war and other factors. Use examples from your study of Health and the People.

(16 marks + 4 marks for SPaG)

Guided War has certainly been a major factor in the development of medicine and public health since medieval times.

....

....

....

....

....

....

....

....

....

....

....

....

....

....

....

....

....

....

....

You should spend about 20 minutes on this answer.

Remember to leave time to write and check your work carefully for **spelling, punctuation and grammar**.

If you start with a strong statement like this, which gets straight to answering the question, you can use it again in your conclusion to give a strong sense of a **sustained line of reasoning and judgement**.

Links You can revise war as a factor in the development of medicine on pages such as 5, 6, 20 and 26–28.

Plan your answer before you start writing. List some ideas which support the idea that war **has** been the main factor; then list other factors that go against the statement:

Support	Against
Even as early as the Middle Ages, war was helping to spread new ideas in medicine through doctors coming back from the Crusades.	Without technology, developments made during wars would not have come to much. For example, penicillin would never have been mass-produced without the technology developed by Hutchinson Rousseau, and blood transfusion might not have been widespread if refrigerators which could store blood for use later hadn't been invented.
Great advances in surgery and drugs were made during the First and Second World Wars.	

Practice

Use this page to continue your answer to question 4.

....
....
....
....
....
....
....
....
....
....
....
....
....
....
....
....
....
....
....
....
....
....
....
....
....

Remember to bring in specific facts and **details** into your answer to show how well you understand the role that **different factors** played in the development of medicine and public health.

Choose the other factors you mention with care – there won't be time to cover them all.

You could say how other factors were important (or even more important) in **relation to the factor in the question**. For example, war was important but without science and technology nothing that scientists came up with during wars would have been developed in a way that drove medicine forward.

Practice

Use this page to continue your answer to question 4.

....
....
....
....
....
....
....
....
....
....
....
....
....
....
....
....
....
....
....
....
....
....
....
....

If you feel really strongly about a factor then don't be afraid to say so.

Try to finish your answer with a **judgement**. It's a good idea to link this back to your opening sentence.

ANSWERS

Where an exemplar answer is given, this is not necessarily the only correct response. In most cases there is a range of responses that can gain full marks.

SUBJECT CONTENT

1. Health and the people

Answers will depend on your own reproductions of the timeline.

Medicine stands still

2. Approaches to disease

For example, one from each of:

Natural:
- using herbal remedies given to them by apothecaries
- burning herbs to rid rooms of the smells people believed caused disease

Supernatural:
- praying to God to forgive sins
- basing diagnoses on astrology
- self-flagellation

3. The medieval doctor
- Schools of Medicine were set up.
- Some doctors would observe their patients and some even tasted their urine to diagnose what was wrong.
- New books were being written by scholars such as Rhazes and read by doctors.

4. Medieval hospitals

1   The hospital was paid for by one man, who must have been rich. Medieval hospitals were often set up by rich people as a way of getting into heaven.
2   Part of the hospital was a chapel, which suggests that it was set up for religious reasons (people believed that charity could cure disease, and would gain them entry into heaven).

5. Religion and medieval medicine

Two ways the Christian Church held medicine back:
- Teaching people that disease came from God, which meant they didn't investigate new ideas.
- Money that could have gone to public health went to religious wars instead.

Two ways the Christian Church moved medicine forward:
- Building and running hospitals, which were very clean and looked after the sick.
- Sending people on the Crusades so they met more skilled and knowledgeable doctors from the Muslim Middle East.

6. Surgery in medieval times

Al-Zahrawi gained his experience of being a surgeon treating soldiers injured in battle. This meant he was able to develop new techniques, painkillers and even instruments. He wrote books on the subject, which as well as being used in Islamic surgery were also shared by European surgeons returning from the Crusades.

7. Towns and monasteries
- In medieval Coventry, the council banned waste disposal in the streets.
- It also ordered toilets built over streams to be knocked down.

8. The Black Death

People thought that the Black Death was a punishment from God for their sins, so they would look for ways of showing God how sorry they were in order to cure the disease or avoid getting it in the first place. The people in the image are whipping themselves to show God how sorry they are. Others might pray for forgiveness.

The beginnings of change

9. Vesalius, Paré and Harvey
- They all challenged the accepted ideas about medicine and the body.
- People opposed their ideas because they didn't like change.

10. Traditional and new methods of treatment

Three from each of the following approaches.

Traditional approaches:
- Quackery (dishonest medical practice)
- Herbal remedies
- Touch from royalty as a cure for 'King's Evil' (scrofula)
- Praying
- Astrology

New approaches:
- More hospitals
- New herbs from around the world
- Family medicine books for home treatments
- Pharmacies
- Scientific approaches

11. The Great Plague

Any three from:
- Both were outbreaks of bubonic plague.
- Both resulted in the deaths of thousands of people.
- Treatment included attempts to balance the Humours by bleeding patients with leeches.
- Cramped and dirty conditions meant the disease spread quickly.
- Religion was still a big part of people's attitudes towards disease.

12. Growth of hospitals
- Specialist hospitals were set up in both periods to treat particular diseases.
- Nurses were employed to care for patients in later hospitals, and a similar role was played by nuns and monks in the Middle Ages.

13. Inoculation and vaccination

At the time people were scared of Jenner's work and didn't take it seriously. They were concerned that smallpox was a punishment from God and people should simply accept it. Also, the people who offered inoculations for a price were worried that they would lose money so set about trying to discredit Jenner.

A revolution in medicine

14. Pasteur
- The microscope allowed for better viewing of microbes.
- The invention of pasteurisation showed that microbes could be killed off – thereby proving they were there in the first place.

15. Koch and microbe hunting

- Koch experimented with the ideas of germ theory to show its accuracy.
- He invented a way of staining bacteria so they could be seen under a microscope.
- His work led many others to important discoveries.

16. Germ theory and vaccination

The cartoon tells me that there was a lot of argument about vaccination. Not everyone was convinced about it because 45 years after compulsory smallpox vaccination was introduced the government decided to let parents who were scared or unsure opt out. The fact that the artist shows this as a triumph for a skeleton (death) also shows that some people thought this was a terrible idea and vaccination should stay compulsory.

17. Ehrlich and magic bullets

The discovery of magic bullets was important because:

- it was the first time a specific germ could be killed, which meant that some illnesses could be cured for the first time
- it was the first time anyone had done large-scale drug research, setting the scene for the modern pharmaceutical industry
- it gave other researchers like Behring the confidence to look for other drugs that would kill specific diseases.

18. Germ theory and everyday medicine

- Developments in vaccination meant that some diseases that would have been widespread, such as diphtheria, almost disappeared.
- Surgery became much safer through the work of people like Lister and Cheyne in improving antiseptic and aseptic surgery.
- Hospitals were much cleaner, making it less likely for patients to get an infection while there.

19. Anaesthetics

- People were frightened by the new anaesthetics, especially as there were many stories of them going wrong.
- People still thought that pain was a punishment from God and it was wrong not to accept it.

20. Antiseptics and aseptic surgery

Lister's ideas led to a big reduction in infection rates and deaths. As they were based on germ theory it showed that the theory was correct and that patients' lives could be saved with attention to cleanliness, confirming that the ideas of other reformers such as Semmelweis and Nightingale were also correct.

21. Industrial Britain

- Towns were usually so dirty that they smelled very bad and this was blamed for disease.
- Most towns were so overcrowded that disease spread very quickly.
- Clean water was in very short supply, and people often used wells and rivers that were contaminated with waste.

22. Public health reformers

For example, one from:

- John Snow's work was important because without it the cholera outbreak of 1854 would have gone on longer and many more people would have died. His work was later used to show that germ theory was correct.
- Edwin Chadwick's work was important because it showed a direct link between poor living conditions and disease. Following his report, the government introduced the 1848 Public Health Act.

23. Government involvement

The government had to change its laissez-faire approach because:

- terrible deadly epidemics made people angry and demand change
- giving more people the vote meant there were more people to pressure the government into acting
- pressure was put on the government by the work of people like John Snow in showing how poor public health policies had led to disease.

Modern medicine

24. Developments in drugs

Both chance and war were important factors in the development of penicillin. If it hadn't been for Fleming's chance finding of mould on a Petri dish, penicillin may never have been discovered. During the Second World War the American government saw the potential of penicillin as a drug to treat its wounded soldiers; without this, penicillin may never have gone into mass-production.

25. New diseases and treatments

- Joseph Lister's focus on hand-washing during the early 19th century brought down infection rates in his surgery; in the same way, it is helping today in the fight against MRSA.
- Florence Nightingale pushed for better cleanliness in hospitals to fight infection, just as the NHS is doing now.

26. Developments in surgery

War was important in the development of surgery in the 20th century in a number of ways. It was during the First World War that major developments were made in orthopaedic and neurosurgery owing to the need to treat bigger, more complex injuries. Blood transfusion machines were developed during the same period, then during the Second World War methods of storing blood were invented. The Second World War also had an important role to play in the development of plastic surgery and of penicillin. Penicillin might not have been developed and mass-produced if it hadn't been for the US government wanting to find a way to treat large numbers of soldiers with infections.

27. Liberal social reforms

The struggle to recruit healthy young men to fight in the Second Boer War shocked the country. Around a third of men who volunteered weren't fit for soldiering and the country was worried that when a bigger war came along it would be difficult to find men to fight. Something had to be done about this so the government introduced public health reforms to try to improve the health of people before the next war.

28. Impact of war

- The people and government wanted to provide homes fit for soldiers who had fought in a terrible war.
- The health of recruits was still very bad and poor quality private rental housing was one of the main reasons.

29. The Welfare State and the NHS

Doctors were against the NHS because they didn't want to be employees of the state. They charged fees for treating patients privately and wanted to continue doing this.

30. Healthcare in the 21st century

- Hospitals are very expensive to build and run.
- National Insurance does not cover all the costs of treatment.
- The original idea was that treatment would be free, but high costs mean that the NHS needs to charge for some things.

PRACTICE

41. Practice

1 Answers might include some of the following points.
Source A is useful to the historian studying government involvement in 19th century public health improvement because it shows:
- people had realised, thanks to individuals like Snow and Chadwick, that disease could be spread quickly through dirty water
- the government understood that control of sewerage was so important they needed to pass laws to ensure it was done properly
- local authorities were passed responsibility for a number of public health measures at this time including responsibility for sewers.

The usefulness of Source A is limited, though, because it doesn't show the following:
- This was one in a series of Acts aimed at improving public health going back to 1834, so the government had been trying to improve public health for nearly half a century.
- This Act also gave local authorities responsibility for things like providing clean drinking water, public toilets and collecting rubbish in a bid to improve public health.
- The effect of this Act (and others) was to greatly reduce outbreaks of diseases such as cholera.

43. Practice

2 Answers might include some of the following points.
Magic bullets were significant in the development of medicine because:
- for the first time specific diseases could be cured through drugs targeting the specific germs which caused them
- it was the first time anyone had done large-scale experimenting in drug research. This work was the foundation of the modern drug industry
- Ehrlich is a good example of how an individual can make a huge difference in medicine
- by 1914 magic bullets had been discovered to attack some of the most prevalent diseases of the time, including syphilis and malaria
- Ehrlich was trained by Koch and the development of magic bullets gave other scientists like Behring the confidence to look for other drugs to target specific diseases. This shows that great individuals working together and building on each other's knowledge was key to development in medicine.

45. Practice

3 Answers might include some of the following points.
In the Middle Ages:
- towns were not particularly clean but some, such as Coventry, did try to clean things up, because they understood that unclean conditions led to disease (although they didn't know why). They did this by:
  - banning the dumping of rubbish in the streets and rivers
  - demolishing toilets built over streams to stop contamination of drinking water
  - banning butchers from slaughtering animals in the streets
  - when there were outbreaks such as Black Death, taking measures to keep the sick away from those not infected.
- hospitals were often quite clean thanks to the religious personnel who ran them and their belief that to be clean was holy.

By 1875:
- the link between unclean conditions and disease was well established and the government passed a number of laws to clean up towns. For example:
  - John Snow had proved the connection between cholera and contaminated water and so eventually measures were taken to improve provision of clean water and make disposal of sewerage safer.
  - The 1848 Public Health Act set up a Board of Health and gave local authorities the right to appoint a Medical Officer for Health with the aim of cleaning up towns.
  - The 1875 Public Health Act required local authorities to clean up towns further with rules about sewerage, clean water provision and clearing rubbish from the streets.
- hospitals were also much cleaner than they had been since medieval times as the work of Florence Nightingale and others was put into practice.

47. Practice

4 Answers might include some of the following points.
Evidence to support the suggestion that war has been the factor in the development of medicine and public health:
- Even as early as the Middle Ages, war was helping to spread new ideas in medicine through doctors coming back from the Crusades.
- Most surgeons in medieval and Renaissance times gained their working knowledge of surgery on the battlefields.
- The Second Boer War recruitment crisis highlighted just how unhealthy the population was, leading to public health measures to change this.
- Great advances in surgery and drugs were made during the First and Second World Wars.

Other factors which could be included:
- Individuals who gained experience in war:
  - Hunter
  - Florence Nightingale improved hospitals following experience gained in the Crimean War
  - Florey.
- Science and technology developments which came out of wars:
  - X-rays
  - Blood grouping
  - Surgical instruments
  - Penicillin mass production.

Notes

Published by Pearson Education Limited, 80 Strand, London, WC2R 0RL.

www.pearsonschoolsandfecolleges.co.uk

Text and illustrations © Pearson Education Limited 2017
Typeset and illustrated by Kamae Design, Oxford
Produced by Out of House Publishing
Cover illustration by Eoin Coveney

The rights of Julia Robertson to be identified as author of this work has been asserted by her in accordance with the Copyright, Designs and Patents Act 1988.

First published 2017

20 19 18 17
10 9 8 7 6 5 4 3 2 1

British Library Cataloguing in Publication Data
A catalogue record for this book is available from the British Library

ISBN 978 1 292 20478 9

Printed in Slovakia by Neografia

Acknowledgements

Content written by Rob Bircher, Brian Dowse, Victoria Payne and Kirsty Taylor is included.

The author and publisher would like to thank the following individuals and organisations for permission to reproduce photographs:

(Key: b-bottom; c-centre; l-left; r-right; t-top)

Alamy Stock Photo: Bilwissedition Ltd. & Co. KG 02t, Chronicle 02b, 04t, 19, 20, Granger Historical Picture Archive 03, Purple Marbles York 1 04b, Walker Art Library 05, Lebrecht Music and Arts Photo Library 07, The Print Collector 08, World History Archive 09t, 15r, 16, 17t, 21, Classic Image 09c, Cameni Images 09b, H.S. Photos 10b, The Granger Collection 11, 33, The Keasbury-Gordon Photograph Archive 12t, Interfoto 12c, Pictorial Press Ltd 12b, 17b, 27l, Science History Images 14, 15l, 15c, GL Archive 22tl, 22tr, 22bl, Paul Fearn 22br, American Photo Archive 26, Heritage Image Partnership Ltd 27r, Lordprice Collection 34; **Getty images:** Science & Society Picture Library 10t; **Shutterstock:** Georgios Kollidas 13; **TopFoto:** 28

All other images © Pearson Education

Note from the publisher

Pearson has robust editorial processes, including answer and fact checks, to ensure the accuracy of the content in this publication, and every effort is made to ensure this publication is free of errors. We are, however, only human, and occasionally errors do occur. Pearson is not liable for any misunderstandings that arise as a result of errors in this publication, but it is our priority to ensure that the content is accurate. If you spot an error, please do contact us at resourcescorrections@pearson.com so we can make sure it is corrected.